The Binder and the Server
Triple Canopy

"The Binder and the Server," the outcome of several group discussions among Triple Canopy editors, was written by senior editor Colby Chamberlain and originally appeared in *Art Journal*, vol. 70, no. 4, Winter 2011. This version of the essay was designed by Franklin Vandiver in collaboration with Triple Canopy and published with generous support from Franklin Street Works Press, Stamford, CT.

triplecanopy

FRANKLIN
STREET
WORKS
PRESS

The Binder and the Server
Triple Canopy

01 Lackeys

> **Many young people strangely boast of being "motivated"; they re-request apprenticeships and permanent training. It's up to them to discover what they're being made to serve.**
>
> **—Gilles Deleuze**

At first a convenience, then quickly a conundrum: *Of course* we would publish on the Internet. We came of age with the medium, it was our generation's default. Plus, financially speaking, it remained—and remains, for now—a wheat-paste endeavor: nine dollars a month to hold down a domain name. A magazine devoid of commercial ambitions but prone to literary pretensions no longer needed a George Plimpton to cut a check covering each month's shortfall. No time spent amassing capital, only submissions. No printers, distributors, or post-office officials to wrangle with, only collaborators. *Online*, of course! It was hardly a discussion. But no sooner had we arrived at consensus than the quandaries presented themselves. For starters: though we all spent hours each day scanning screens for information, what on the Internet did we actually *read*?

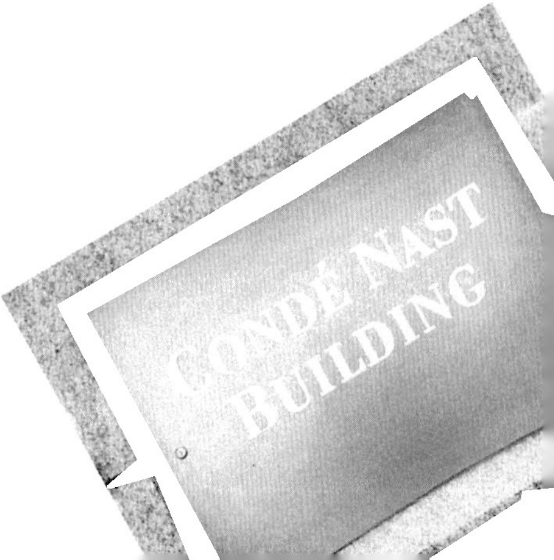

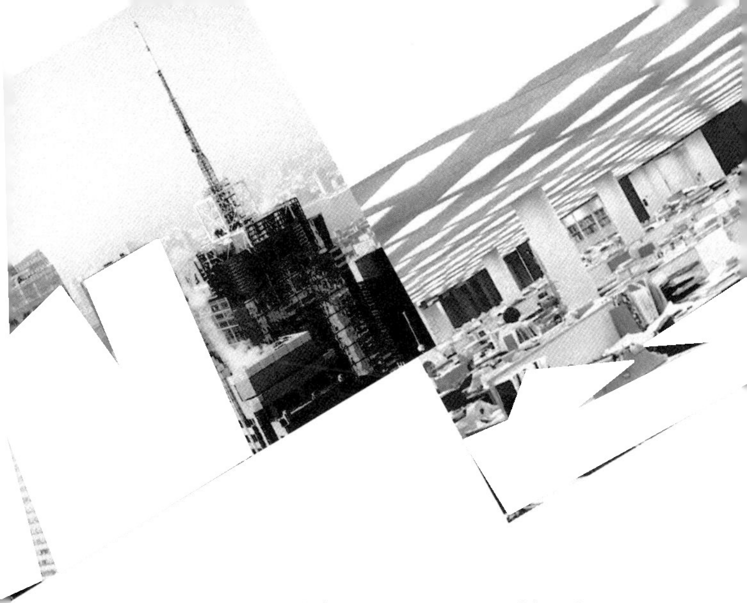

Our loyalties, you see, were split. The Internet was the air we breathed, but print paid the bills. Many of us were fledgling contributors, fact-checkers, editors for publications ranging from *Cabinet* to the heavyweights at Condé Nast. In a draft of a letter soliciting contributions, we identified ourselves as print's lackeys. (One editor's note in tracked changes registers discomfort with the term: "'Lackeys' might not work for everyone, but 'workers' has a nice doubleness?" Fair enough, but often it's the accuracy of a word that engenders uneasiness.) We still subscribed, so to speak, to the notion that a true reading experience depended on the material substrate of a page. Our shift from print to online publishing couldn't be smooth; we had to anticipate, even instigate, some violence in the transfer. We assumed a contradictory stance: embrace the era's technology, but hold it at arm's length. That same solicitation letter contains the first instance of our future mantra:

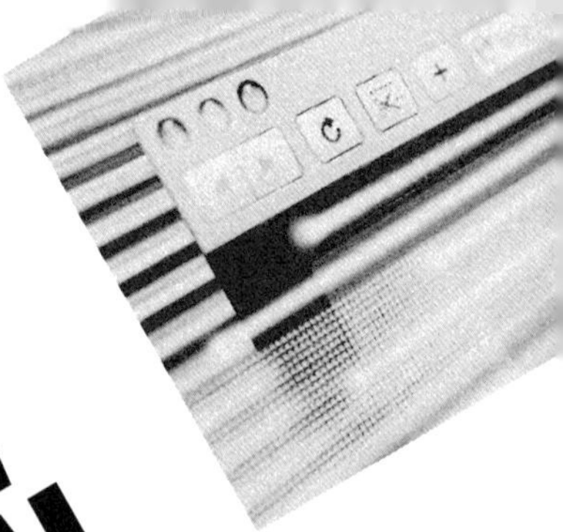

SLOW DOWN THE INTERNET

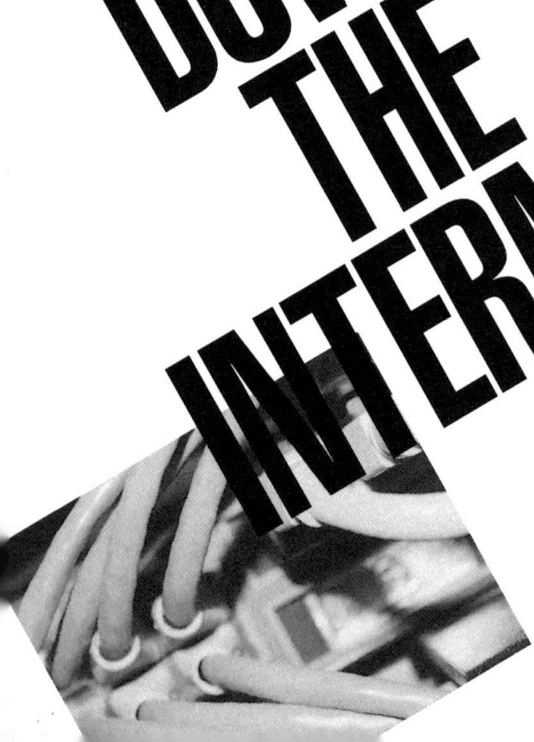

Sorry, we got ahead of ourselves. Proper introductions are still in order. For those of you unfamiliar, we are the editors of Triple Canopy, an online magazine based (where else?) in Brooklyn, with satellites in Los Angeles and Berlin. Since March 2008 we have published fifteen issues and organized public programs from Tucson to Sarajevo. Recently we moved into an office and venue at 155 Freeman Street in Greenpoint, along with the microcinema Light Industry and the open-source classroom The Public School New York. To elaborate:

> Triple Canopy is an online magazine, workspace, and platform for editorial and curatorial activities. Working collaboratively with writers, artists, and researchers, Triple Canopy facilitates projects that engage the Internet's specific characteristics as a public forum and as a medium, one with its own evolving practices of reading and viewing, economies of attention, and modes of interaction. In doing so, Triple Canopy is charting an expanded field of publication, drawing on the history of print culture while acting as a hub for the exploration of emerging forms and the public spaces constituted around them.

We say as much on our grant applications, though with constant revision; apparently, an organization built around a website poses some conceptual difficulties for the review boards that allot funding. If you're a magazine tracing rivulets through literature, the visual arts, and long-form journalism, what "common good" are you providing, and what "public" do you serve? There's no extra credit for delving into questions that thorny when applying to the NEA.

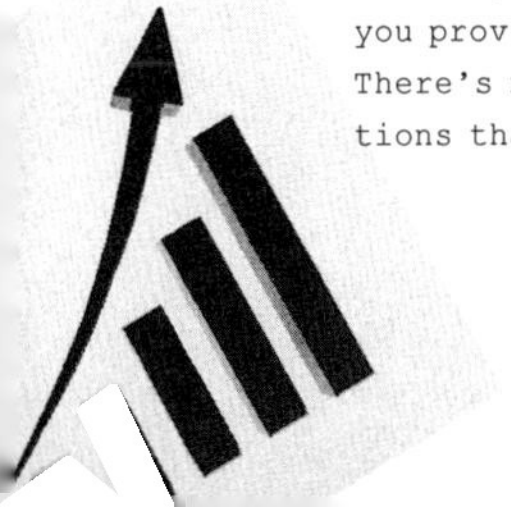

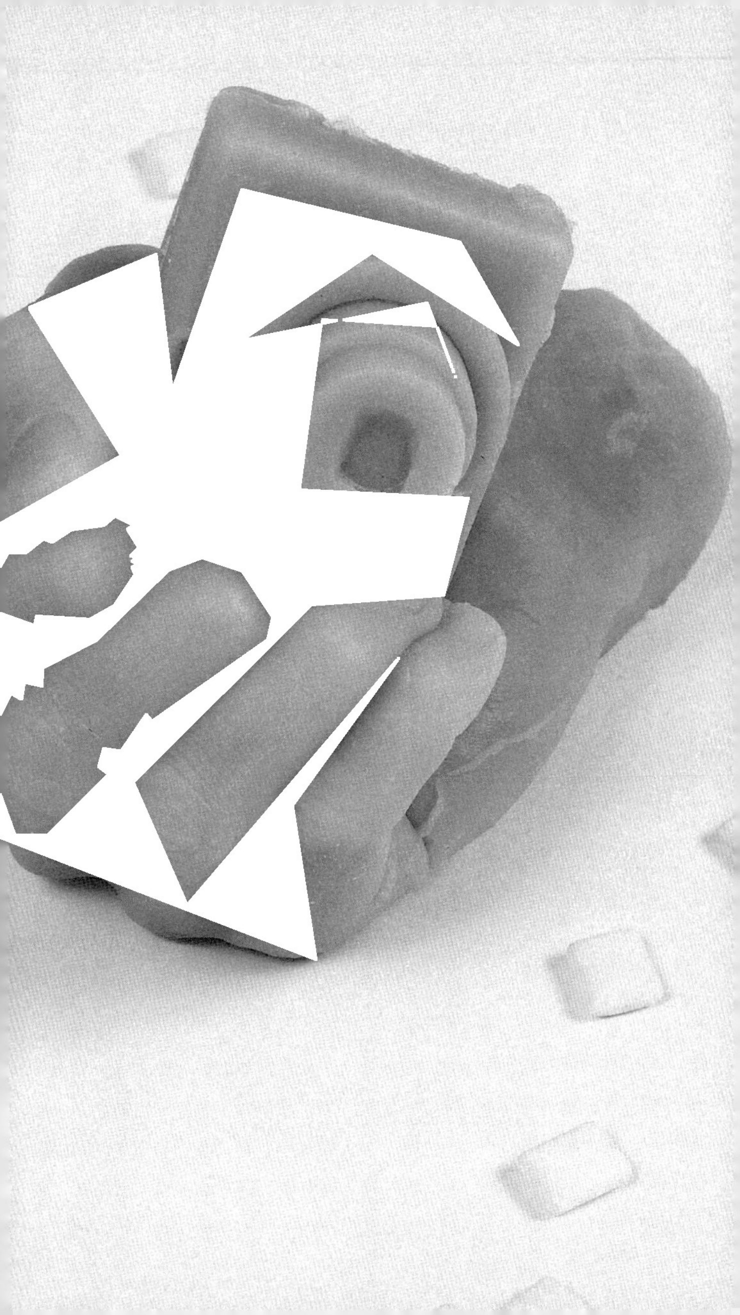

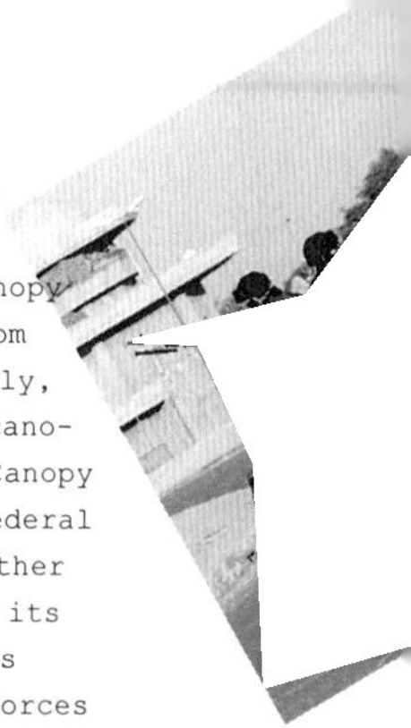

Perhaps our name is causing some confusion. You may have gleaned from the column inches of various newspapers that Triple Canopy is involved in activities quite distinct from online publishing. Indeed, we are, officially, Canopy Canopy Canopy, Inc., and our URL is canopycanopycanopy.com. The legitimate Triple Canopy is a security contractor working with the federal government in Iraq and Afghanistan, among other places, and with corporations based in what its website calls "austere environments." It was founded by veterans of the US Army Special Forces in 2003, presumably to profit from the free-market outsourcing bonanza of the Bush-Cheney administration. In 2009, Triple Canopy was assigned the contracts previously awarded to the firm Blackwater, which had come under scrutiny after a notorious shooting incident in Baghdad. Also, Triple Canopy is hiring. We know these things because they show up in our Google Alerts.

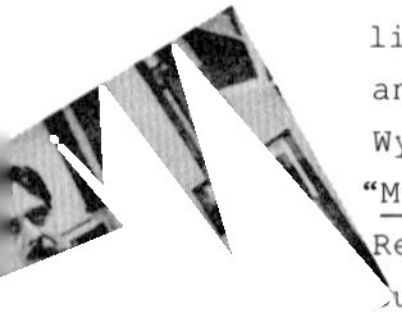

So we appropriated the strangely beautiful name of a vaguely sinister enterprise. It felt like the right decision for a nation that was, and still is, at war. Maybe we were thinking of Wyndham Lewis's caustic proclamation in *Blast*: "Mercenaries were always the best troops."[1] Regardless, it turns out that the choice of our name was more accurate, more *medium-specific*, than we could have anticipated. In part, we founded an online magazine to engineer our release from lackey status into independence; but even if we're no longer lackeys, we're not exactly free agents either. That was always an impossibility. The pressing question in this essay is whether the shift from print to online publishing actually signals any major transformation. Well, in short, yes. It's going to take us the rest of this article to explain in full, but it comes down to this:

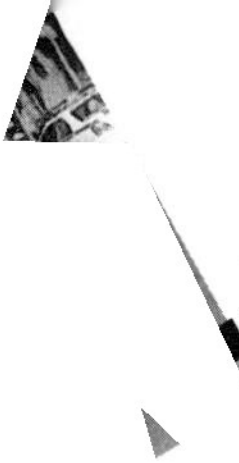

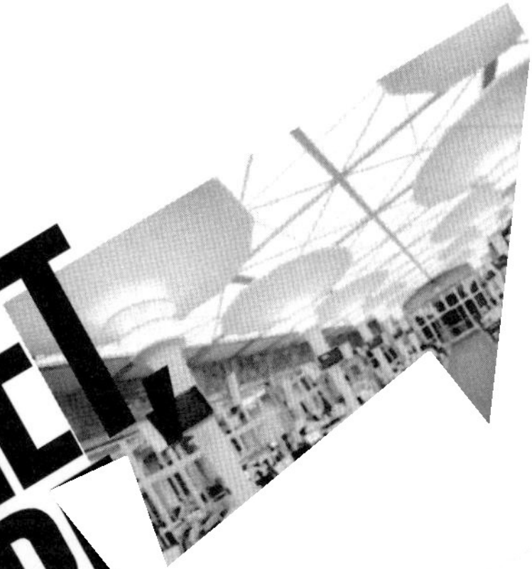

ON THE INTERNET, WE ARE ALL CONTRA- CTORS.

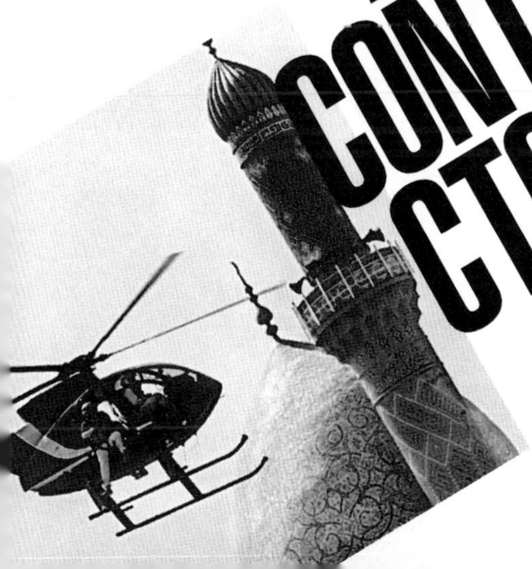

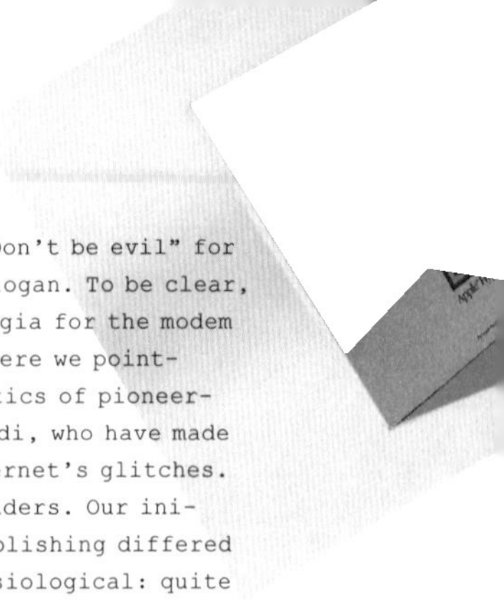

Slow down the Internet. Like "Don't be evil" for Google, this was our guiding slogan. To be clear, we didn't coin it out of nostalgia for the modem blips of the dial-up era. Nor were we pointing toward the saboteur aesthetics of pioneering Net artists like the duo Jodi, who have made a career of exploiting the Internet's glitches. Rather, we were speaking as readers. Our initial conviction that online publishing differed from print was practically physiological: quite simply, our eyes moved differently over screens. Some of that saccadic strain was the unavoidable consequence of the technological support, but widespread tendencies in web design were equally culpable. The entire Internet seemed convulsed by *horror vacui*, with surfaces cluttered and margins covered. We always found our attention yanked toward some errant blinking in our peripheral vision, or to another site entirely. Repeatedly, reading deteriorated into skimming. This phenomenon wasn't limited to text; any images, audio, or video that demanded sustained attention fared equally poorly. To slow down the Internet, we wanted to reproduce the absorptive experience that print still afforded us, while also incorporating the web's capacity for interactivity and multiple media. The trick was to achieve this mix in a manner somehow centripetal, so that diverse elements mutually reinforced the reader's focus instead of scattering it.

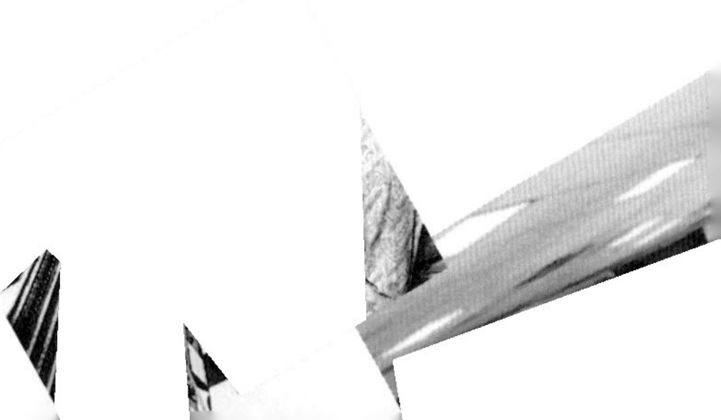

Of course, this was all aspirational blather until our creative director Caleb Waldorf and senior web developer Adam Florin created Triple Canopy's original platform. When they debuted their prototype for the website, those of us less technically adept were astonished: a whole intellectual position was here elegantly articulated in code. The principal feature was a rectangular frame that held each article's content. To the left and right of the frame were a minus and plus sign, respectively. Clicking the plus sign carried you through the piece, one frame of content at a time. It was a succinct digital equivalent to flipping pages, only those "pages" could support text, full-bleed images, audio, video, and interactive graphics with equal ease. (A custom content-management system allowed editors to design articles using a number of templates, requiring only rudimentary knowledge of HTML.) The conceit was a synthesis of the printed magazine and Hypercard, an important precursor to today's web browsers; the strategy was to focus attention on an article's content by eliminating any extraneous elements; the kicker, we all agreed, was the horizontal movement. In contrast to the Internet's default of vertical scrolling, which originated as a way for programmers to sift through massive amounts of code *without* reading and which encourages eyes to jump, skim, and stray, the left-to-right progress provided subtle cues that a proper reading experience was under way. The platform was novel and familiar in equal measure, both an anomaly in web design and a throwback to print. Reanimating the dead metaphor of the web "page," it was undeniably *retardataire* but—we hoped—radically so.

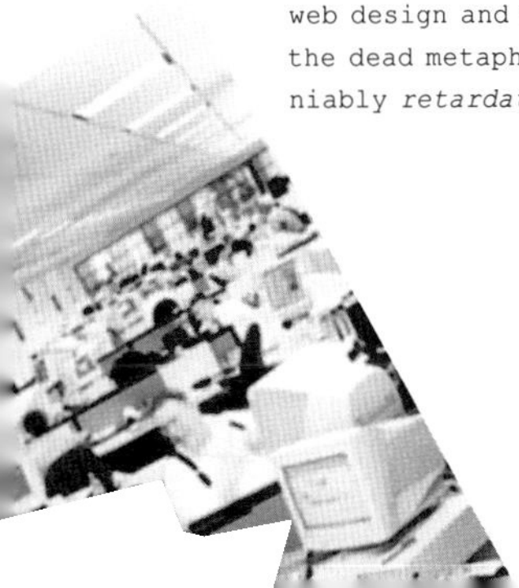

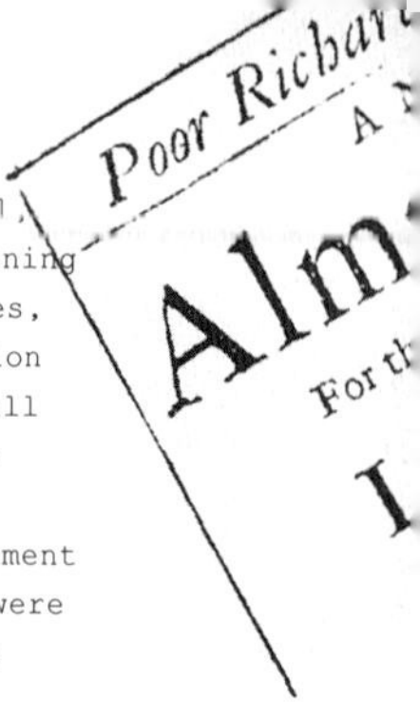

Then we published our first issue. (Well, not *right then*; obviously there were intervening steps like commissioning and editing articles, and so on, but for the purposes of this section we're restricting the narrative to our overall conception for the website, OK?) Promptly we discovered the flaw in our thinking. We had developed our response to the online environment from the perspective of readers, but now we were producers—and distributors to boot. Imagine if magazines had detailed information about everyone who picked up an issue at a newsstand, flipped through the pages, then placed it back on the rack. We do. Visits to our site get logged in Google Analytics, and if we want to know the number of articles accessed by people reading for four minutes or longer in southern Ohio who found us by searching for "logical stories," it's a simple query. After publishing all fourteen articles of our first issue at once on March 17, 2008, we monitored our analytics compulsively, and often what they revealed was excruciating. We saw how the page-views spiked after our mass e-mail announcing the release, then fell off drastically when we didn't add new content in the days following. We saw the navigation problems, how readers of one article seldom found their way back to the table of contents to select another. We had the precise count of everyone who stayed for less than two minutes before they bounced away. It's one thing to know in the abstract that people likely leaf through your magazine and quickly lose interest; it's quite another to have a comprehensive record of this occurring daily across the globe.

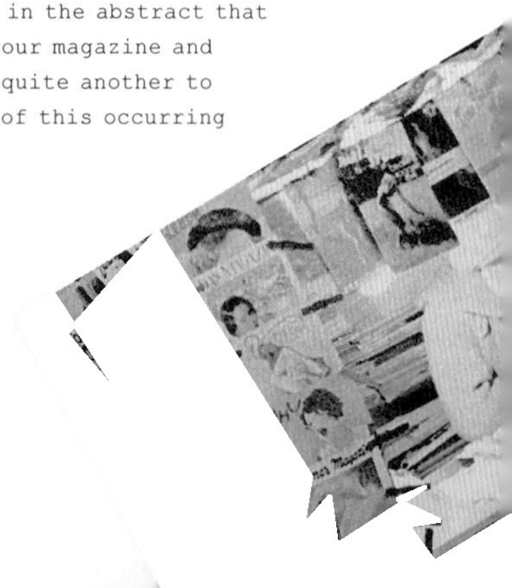

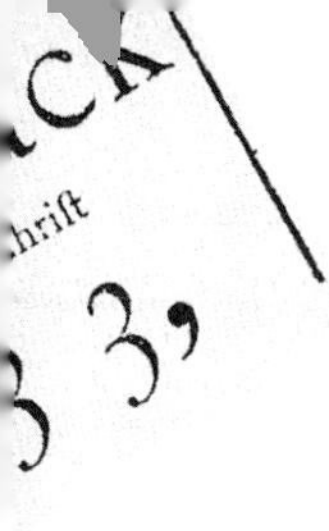

At the same time, our central conceit—the foregrounding of the page—was posing technical challenges. These extended beyond the inevitable bugs and glitches that accompany any site launch; they were structural. Our magazine, you see, had two sets of readers, and those first and foremost had names like Firefox, Safari, and Explorer. Browser applications turned the source code into content, and each possessed slightly different standards for font size and spacing. The resulting discrepancies fractured the fixed units of our pages. A paragraph that fit comfortably on a page in Firefox 4.1 would run over in Safari 3.6, creating odd breaks or throwing off the position of an image. There was no sure-fire method of preventing these errors, so instead we tested each article in multiple browsers on PCs and Macs. We patrolled for flaws and fiddled with code. Unwittingly we had replicated one of print publishing's most finicky aspects, the last-minute fussing over hyphens and page breaks at press check—only for us it was a perpetual process. In our effort to slow down the Internet, we ourselves became mired in tedium.

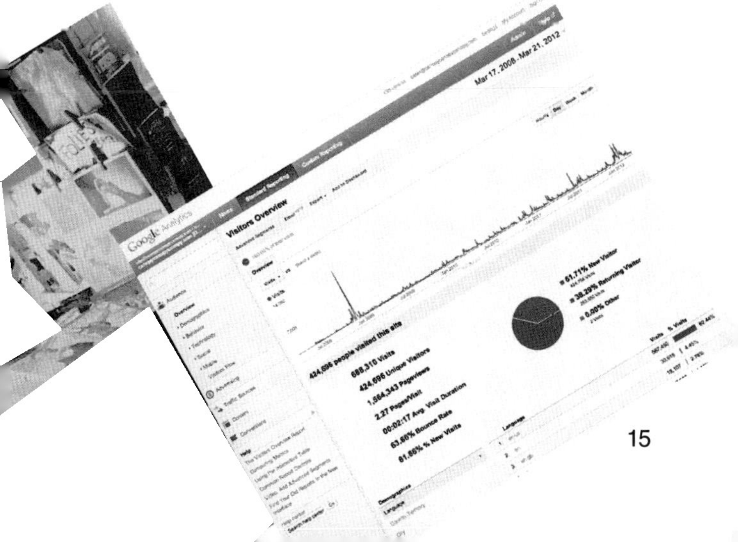

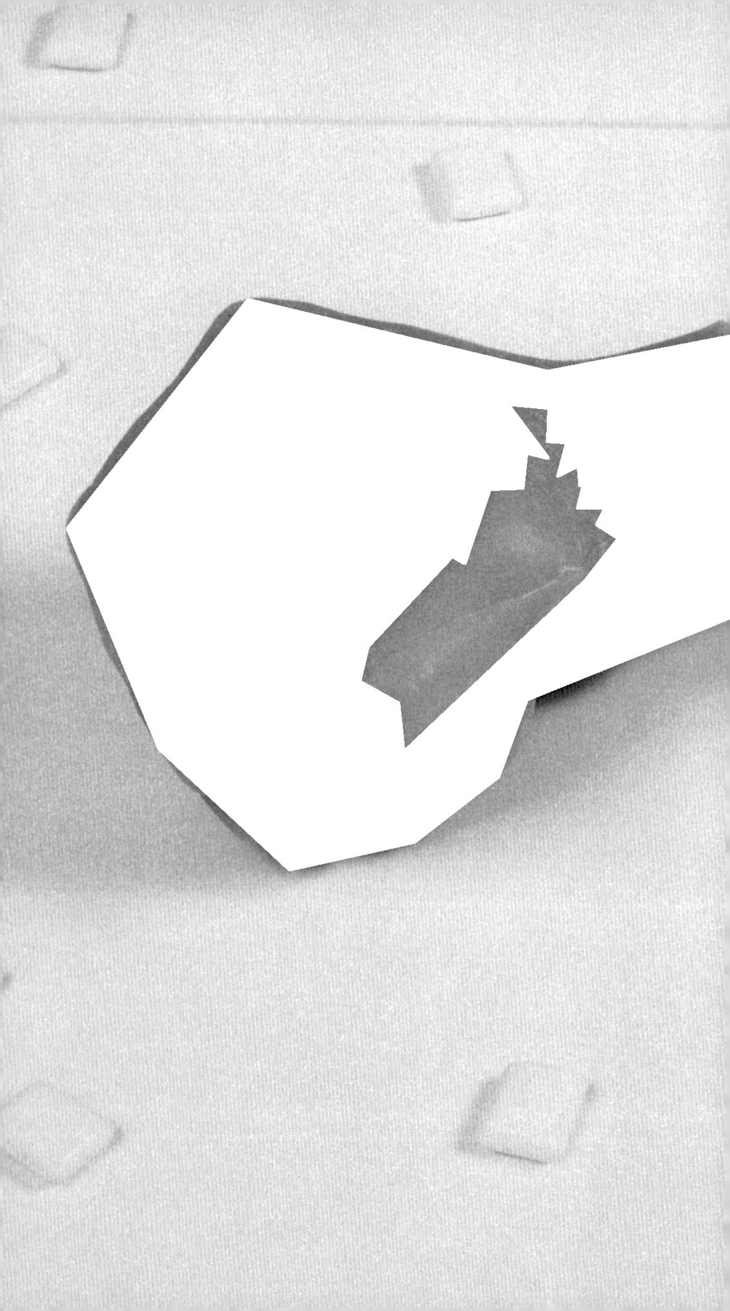

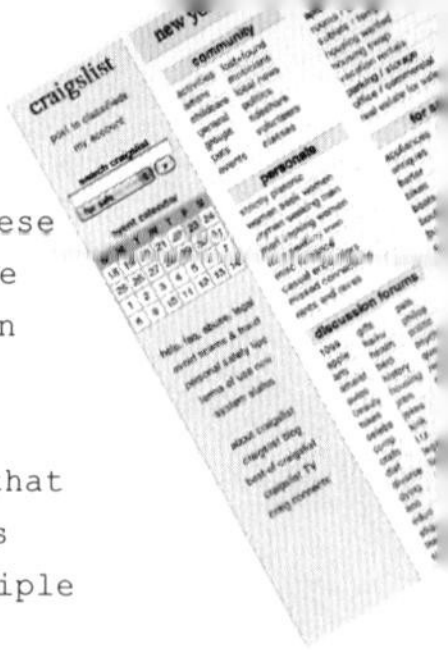

What was happening? We could explain these challenges one by one, but that would obscure the bigger picture. Here it's helpful to turn to the theorist and programmer Alexander R. Galloway's important book *Protocol*, which examines the technical rules and standards that govern relationships across the Internet. As much as Waldorf and Florin's code for the Triple Canopy platform encapsulated our collective conversation and engendered a particular kind of reading experience, so too does the underlying programming of the entire Internet reflect a widespread consensus and dictate a fixed model of behavior.

SOME ASPECTS OF PROTOCOL ARE QUITE RIGID, OTHERS INCREDIBLY FLEXIBLE

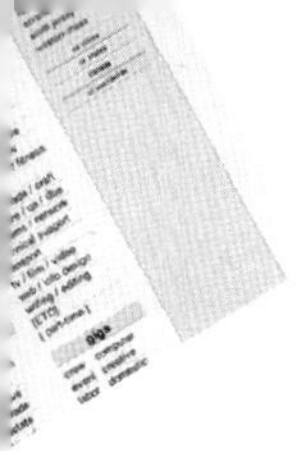

Access to the Internet is available to all, but that access is contingent on conforming to specific technical standards, or protocols. These are the rules and recommendations that govern how web addresses are structured, or determine how information packets travel from one computer to another, or outline what HTML tags browsers need to interpret a page correctly.

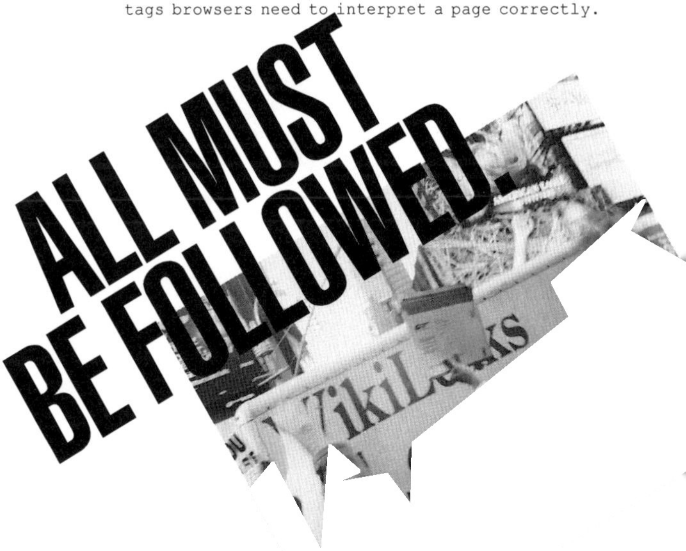

"In order for protocol to enable radically distributed communications between autonomous entities, it must employ a strategy of universalization, and of homogeneity," writes Galloway. "It must be anti-diversity. It must promote standardization in order to enable openness."[2] All this is achieved through self-regulation by individual participants, which makes for a curious system of governance.

EVERYONE OBEYS THE RULES

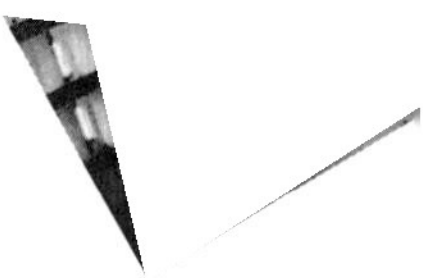

Nothing in the programming of Triple Canopy's original website broke absolutely with protocol, yet by trying to lock text into the specific dimensions of our pages, we had strayed from standardization. Source code doesn't furnish browsers with a layout but rather instructions for one; a web page is created anew each time someone asks to view it. Vertical scrolling became the norm in part because it could easily accommodate these serial instances of interpretation. Our programming aspired to an ideal design, whereas the Internet generally privileged variation and difference. If we had published our magazine on paper and discovered inconsistencies from one copy of an issue to the next, obviously we would complain to our printers until they fixed it. When publishing online and encountering the same problem, there was no one to petition. Who was even responsible? We had no recourse but to regulate ourselves: troubleshooting, trial-and-error, learning to avoid certain layouts, anxiously reevaluating after each major upgrade to popular browsers. Et cetera.

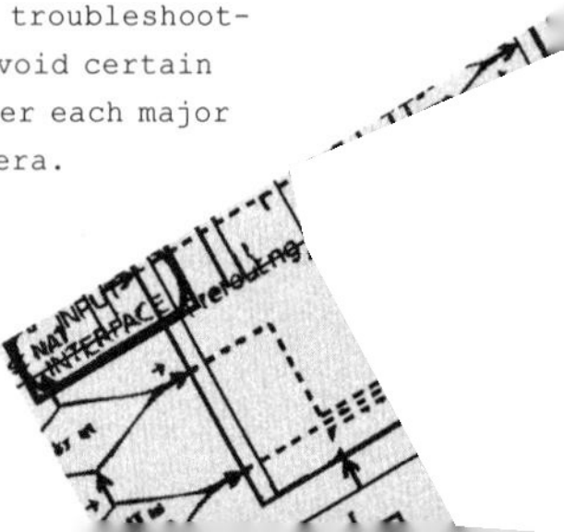

For our tenth issue, published in November 2010, we overhauled the platform's programming entirely, in part to address this ongoing annoyance in a comprehensive manner. A major change in conception lay at the redesign's core: we broke apart the page. We retained the horizontal scroll that felt so intrinsic to the Triple Canopy reading experience, but eliminated the strict page breaks that had caused so many glitches. A smaller unit, the column, became our organizing principle; now when the reader clicks the plus sign, the text advances by a single column. In the vocabulary we developed for the new code, we distinguished between flowing elements, like text, and floating ones, like slideshows and video. In both cases, content was unmoored from the fixed page. Precise placement mattered less. Our layout became flexible and fluid—in other words, far more to protocol's liking. In order to achieve greater consistency, we gave up a degree of control.

BUT NO ONE NFORCES THEM.

To help explain our second set of early challenges—namely, all that anxiety-producing data Google Analytics kept feeding us—we need to move past protocol, but stay in its domain. Galloway's theoretical model for *Protocol* is heavily indebted to Gilles Deleuze's tantalizingly brief (or frustratingly underdeveloped, depending on your disposition) "Postscript on the Societies of Control." The essay argues that the enclosed institutions of Foucault's discipline society—the barracks, the school, the prison—have given way to the continuous, open-ended topologies of what Deleuze calls control societies. Power is no longer exercised at fixed coordinates along clear lines of force; rather, power is pervasive and operates subtly. Instead of bowing to disciplinary procedures, autonomous agents internalize their directives. For Galloway, computer protocol is a prime example of control at work; everything on the Internet follows regulations despite the lack of punitive measures. The logic of control is one of constant self-modulation. Often what regulates this process is a steady flow of statistics. In control societies, persons are broken down into aggregates of information (Social Security numbers, shopper IDs, checking accounts, IP addresses, biometrics, genetic code, and so on). "Individuals have become '*dividuals*,' and masses, samples, data, markets, or '*banks*.'"[3]

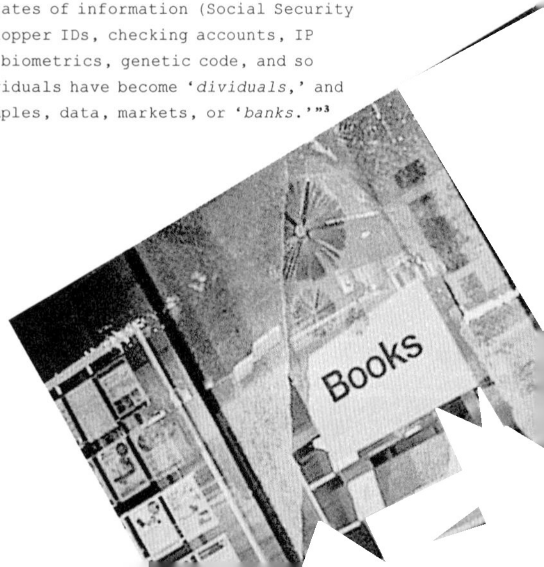

In the case of Triple Canopy's first issue, the magazine had individual readers—say, the friends who shared their first impressions with us—but an order of magnitude more *dividuals*, i.e., the numerous points of data compiled by Google Analytics. The statistical patterns we found nudged us to make changes. For instance, whereas we had published our first issue all at once, for subsequent issues we posted articles two or three times per week over the course of a month, in closer sync with the Internet's regular clip of updated content.

When the data indicated visitors seldom found their way to a second article, we started to fill the abundant blank space of our initial design with links and navigation tools. Here we had entered a feedback loop, making frequent minute adjustments in response to changes in statistical results. (Through this process we were also conditioning our visitors, continually acclimating them to the unfamiliar experience of reading a lengthy article online.) Nothing obliged us to make these departures from our original conception for the platform, yet we did so anyway. That's the paradox of control:

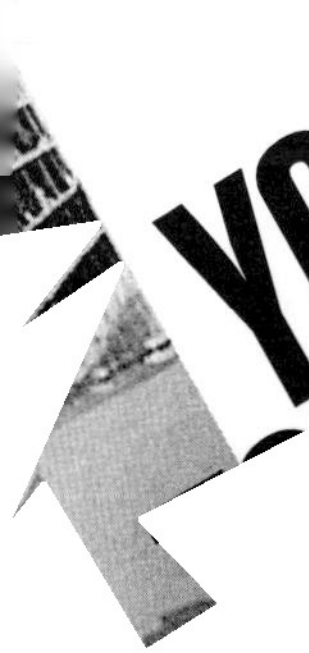

YOU WANT
DO WHAT IT
WANTS YOU
TO DO.

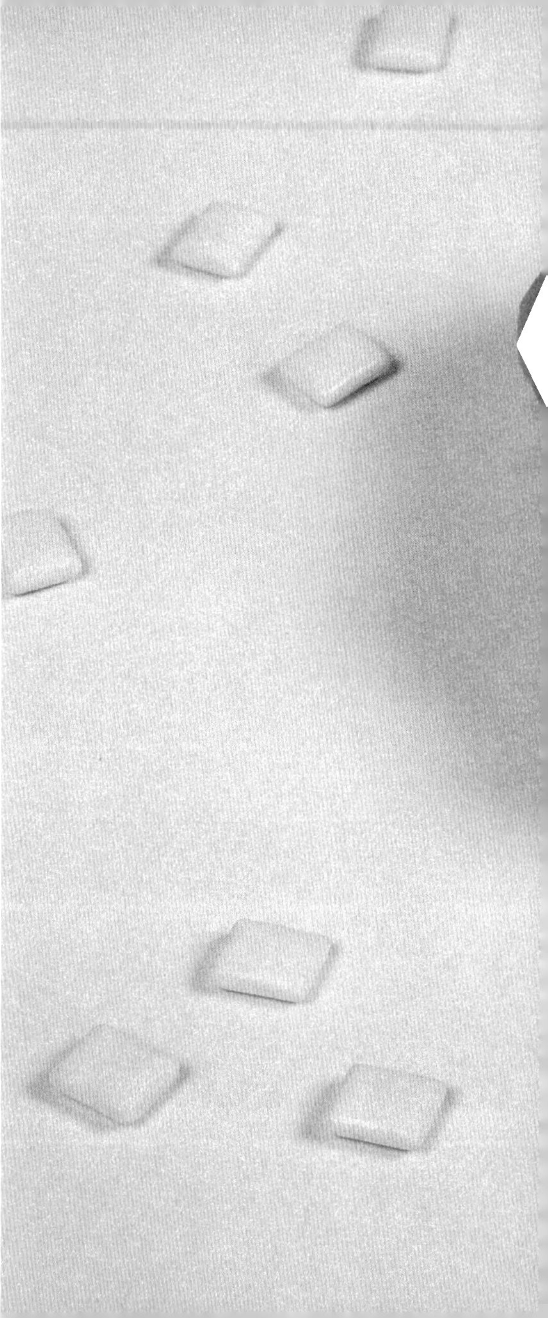

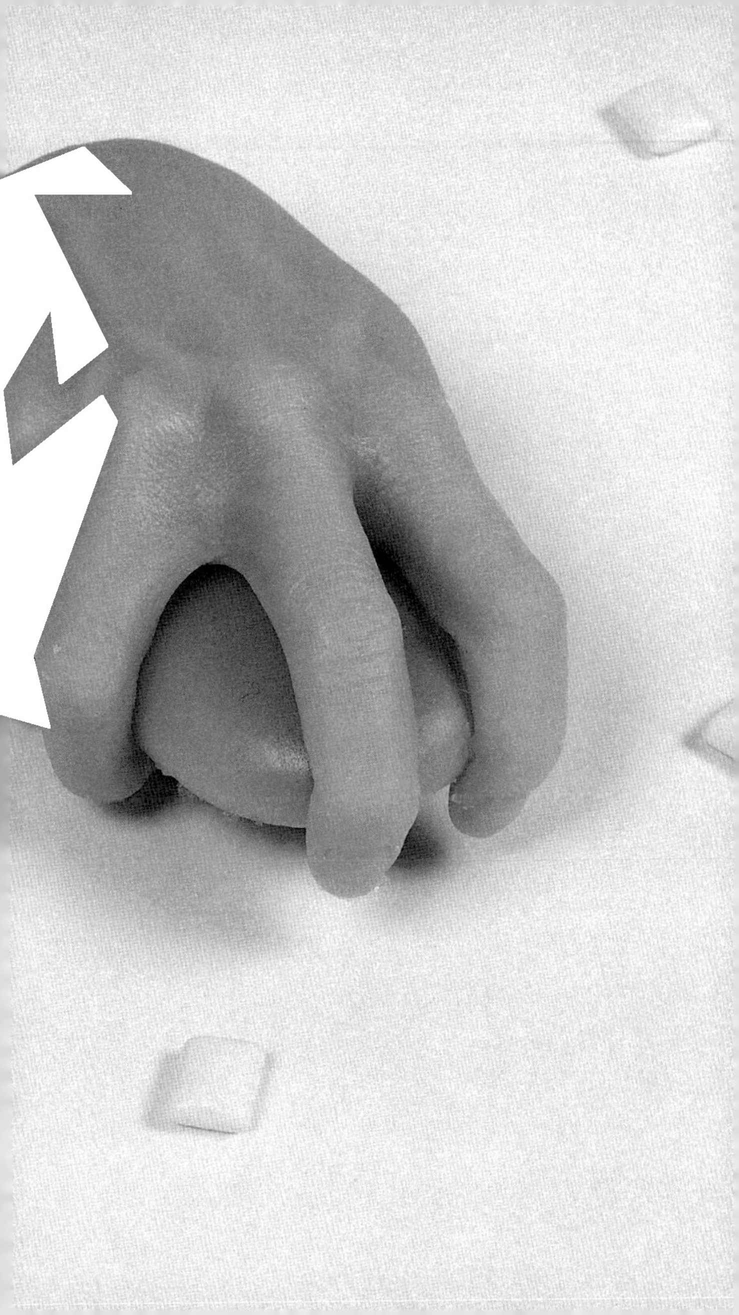

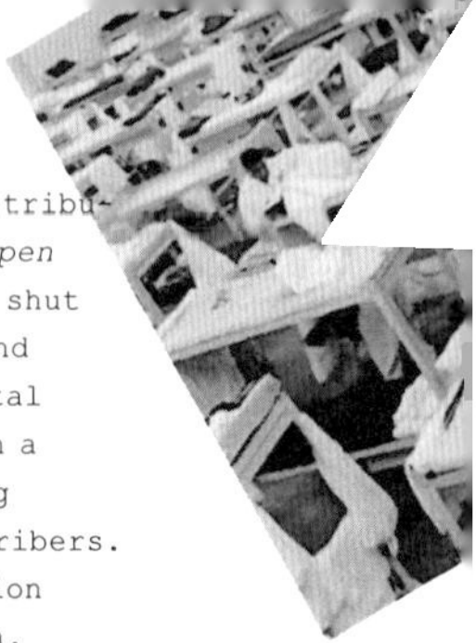

Let's reframe: For any magazine, distribution entails obligation. Notoriously, *Aspen* (1965–71) lost its periodical status and shut down because its irregular publication and changing format failed to conform to postal regulations. To this day, the pressure on a magazine to maintain a regular publishing schedule comes from newsstands and subscribers. As a website, our capacity for distribution far exceeds that of any print publication, especially those offbeat or recondite "little magazines" that, in sensibility, we consider close peers. Yet the technical possibility of reaching several million readers at little cost is hardly free—so far as "free will" is concerned. Publishing online involves a subtle, steady stream of particular considerations, self-corrections, unacknowledged concessions that affect everything from the juxtaposition of text and video within articles to our overarching vision of the project.

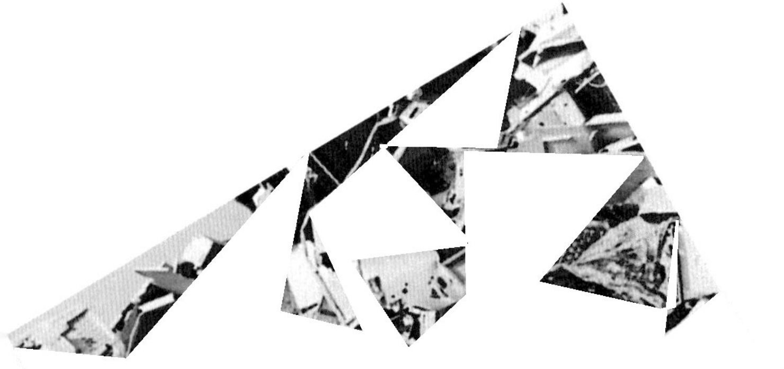

For a print magazine, everything occurs in discrete spatial units: it handles content and design in-house, then brings that material to a press for production, then contracts out distribution to other agencies, including the postal service. For those of us who once worked for print magazines, the single moment when distribution became a serious preoccupation was the selection of a cover image, since that's what attracts casual browsers in bookstores; the inside contents were animated by other concerns. For online publications, the sites of distribution and production are continuous. The nature of search and hyperlinks is that new visitors are just as likely to come across the magazine via a specific article as the landing page. However much we wanted Triple Canopy's platform to counteract the entrenched reading habits of the Internet, we also wanted first-time users to understand intuitively how to engage with our content. Our 2010 redesign was a provisional reconciliation of those two competing desires.

To summarize: From our perspective, print magazines still have room to maneuver, to be oppositional, contrary, *outside*. There's a discrete place for free play removed from whatever strictures distributors and advertisers might impose. For an online magazine, there is no outside. Instead there is protocol, analytics, feedback loops. Slowing down the Internet, it turns out, isn't an oppositional stance, but a continually negotiated one. "*Opposing protocol is like opposing gravity—there is nothing that says it can't be done, but such a pursuit is surely misguided and in the end hasn't hurt gravity much.*"[4]

That's all one way of explaining the departures from our initial platform, one way of parsing the distinctions between print and online publishing. There's a whole other narrative arc that's equally relevant, one that we won't dwell on here because you're already aware of it. Since our debut issue in 2008, a tremendous amount of capital has been expended turning screens into pages, often in a manner so dishearteningly literal that the column units of our redesign became a more appealing option. Amazon's Kindle, Barnes & Noble's Nook—we shudder to think of the millions spent on rendering the animation of a page being flipped *just so*.

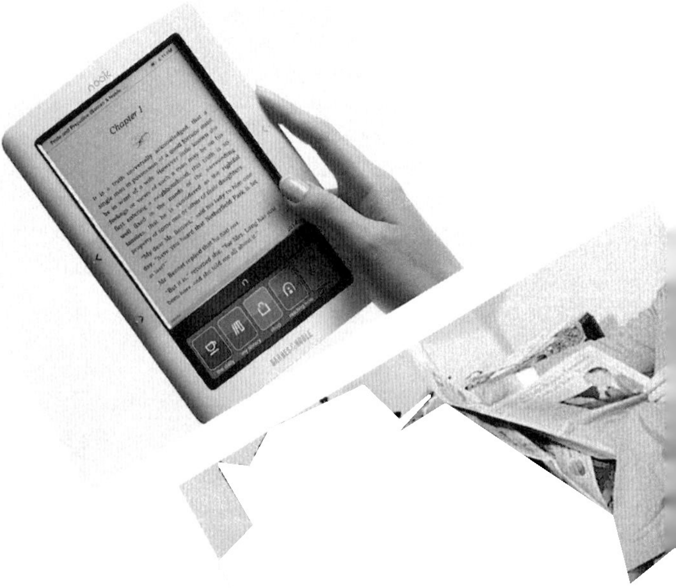

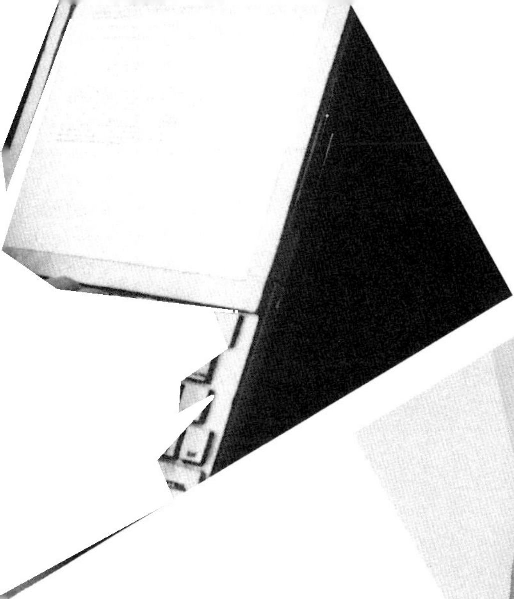

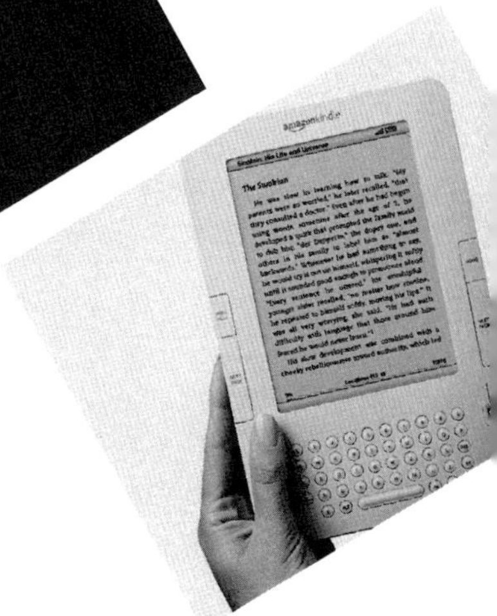

Meanwhile, mass-market magazines have realized they compromised their revenue models by posting free content online and are now rushing toward subscription applications for the iPad—proprietary for-pay software that binds users to an interface that is severed from the rest of the web. We see this as a reactionary move, as a strike against the Internet's capacity for connectivity. It's only mildly hyperbolic to claim that such "apps" represent an attempt to reestablish a segment of the disciplinary society—the digital equivalent of the barracks, an enclosed space for readers with aspects of both the department store and the prison house. Those who held sway in the old dispensation are growing nervous, and they're stocking up for a long siege.

Open Letter to Kevin Kelly

Hi Kevin,

How are things? We've been meaning to write for a while—since 2008, actually, when you posted an article of ours to your (widely read!) blog. You remember, right? "Star Wars: A New Heap," by John Powers, that elaborate Smithson-inspired disquisition on the relationship between *Star Wars* and Minimalist sculpture. Apparently sci-fi is the Internet's main artery, because we've never gotten more unique hits for any article. No doubt your endorsement sent some eyeballs our way. "It is one of the densest, highest ideas-per-page reads I've had in a long time," you wrote. We copied that and put it on our press page—out of context, so it seems you're referring to the magazine as a whole, not just a single article. We hope you don't mind. Hell, just about any movie poster with critics' blurbs has done worse, right? Thanks so much!

But anyway, we finally got around to writing because we've been reading your new book, *What Technology Wants*. You are, after all, an eminence grise of this unwieldy networked era in which we find ourselves—an early contributor to the *Whole Earth Software Catalog* in the 1980s, a founding editor of *Wired* in the 1990s—so it seems as if we should be paying attention to what you say. Your central argument, as far as we can tell, is that fixating on the development and impact of specific technologies misses the big picture. Instead we should focus on what you call "the technium," a vital energy vibrating all around us. "The technium is now as great a force in our world as nature, and our response to the technium should be similar to our response to nature." If we conceive of the technium as a natural system, we'll be able to discern the patterns of technology's evolution and discern what it wants: efficiency, opportunity, diversity, sentience, beauty (and on from there; your list is quite long). "By following what technology wants, we can be more ready to capture its full gifts."[5] That's all well and good, but the thing is, we couldn't help thinking we had read about what technology wants and how to service its needs before, in terms that weren't quite so rosy. We thumbed through our libraries till we found it:

> It means this War was never political at all, the politics was all theater, all just to keep the people distracted ... secretly it was being dictated instead by the needs of technology ... by a conspiracy between human beings and techniques, by something that needed the energy-burst of war, crying, "Money be damned, the very life of [insert name of Nation] is at stake," but meaning, most likely, *dawn is nearly here, I need my night's blood, my funding, funding, ahh more, more....* The real crises were crises of allocation and priority, not among firms—it was only staged to look that way—but among the different Technologies. Plastics, Electronics, Aircraft, and their needs which are understood only by the ruling elite ...[6]

By the ellipses alone, you probably surmised this came from *Gravity's Rainbow*. How did you two arrive at such contrary conceptions of what technology wants? You predict peace and prosperity; Pynchon, perpetual war. Is it just the old saying, one man's technophilia is another man's paranoid dread? Or maybe it's part and parcel of the historical trajectory Fred Turner traces in *From Counterculture to Cyberculture*, where he follows the career path of Stewart Brand to explain how the cultural connotation for computers changed from dehumanizing machines in the early 1960s to a life-affirming means of self-realization in the 1990s? Either way, the juxtaposition underscores what makes us uneasy about your claims. All your recourse to biological metaphor—technological development as species evolution, the technium as the seventh kingdom of life—is a variation on social Darwinism. That is, you attempt to naturalize technology, as if there were no historical actors, as if things couldn't have turned out otherwise. You don't consider how technologies have been mobilized to benefit particular economic or political agendas. The question *Cui bono*? never occurs to you.

What are we trying to say? Yours is a dream of a world without power. In his book, Turner notes that Brand zealously hid from public scrutiny the degree to which control over the *Whole Earth Catalog* was consolidated with him. We wonder if this wasn't an original sin of sorts, considering how influential the *Catalog* proved to be in shaping the popular reception of networked computing in the 1990s. By obscuring the dynamics within his own organization, Brand took the question of power off the table.[7] Power, power was always the dirty secret, and any analysis that fails to account for it has fallen for its ruse. So if we left the study of the Internet to you and your fellow boosters at *Wired*, the "conspiracy between human beings and techniques" would carry on unabated. *My funding, funding, ahh more, more*.... The majority of *Gravity's Rainbow*, you'll remember, takes place in the Zone, that Europe-wide interregnum in the dwindling days of World War II, when national boundaries have dissolved and the main characters shed their allegiances, altering their trajectories and assuming new personae according to their own desires—or so they think, since always they are subjects to power, obeying forces both pervasive and invisible. Sounds like we're all in the Zone now.

Thanks again!

Three Cheers,
Triple Canopy

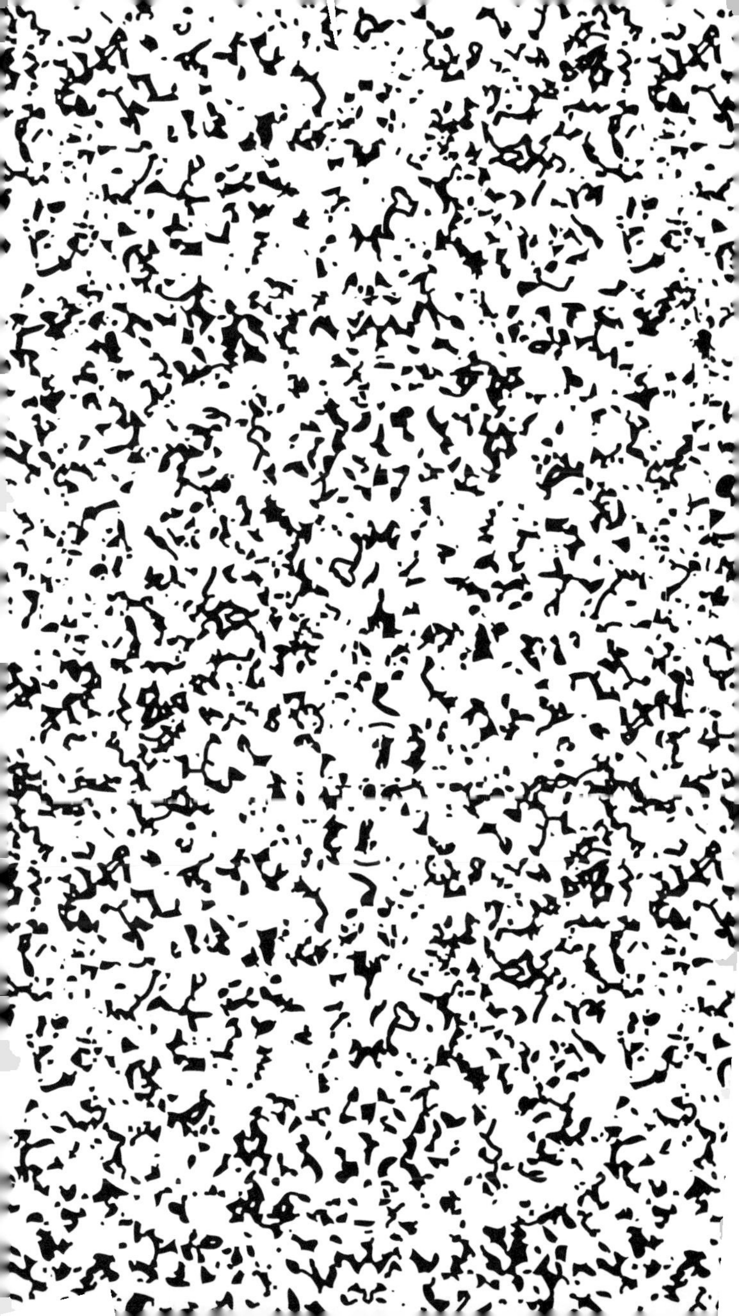

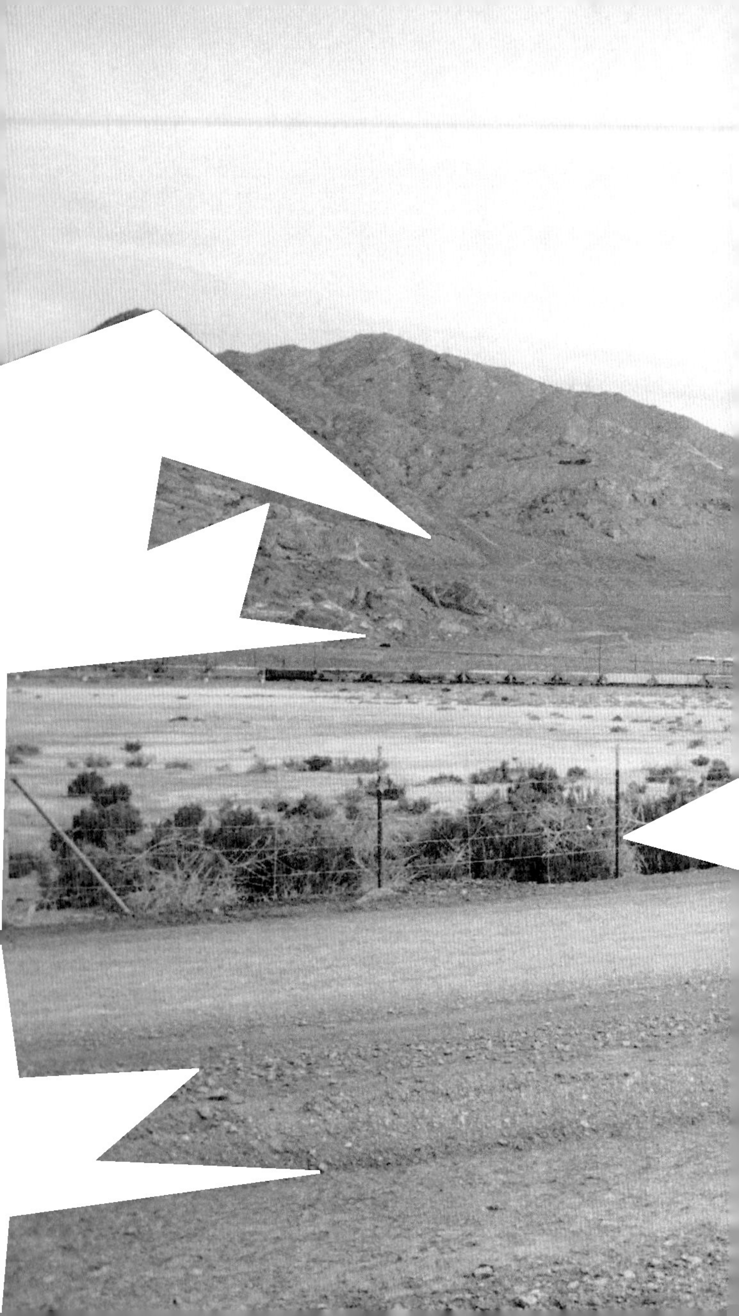

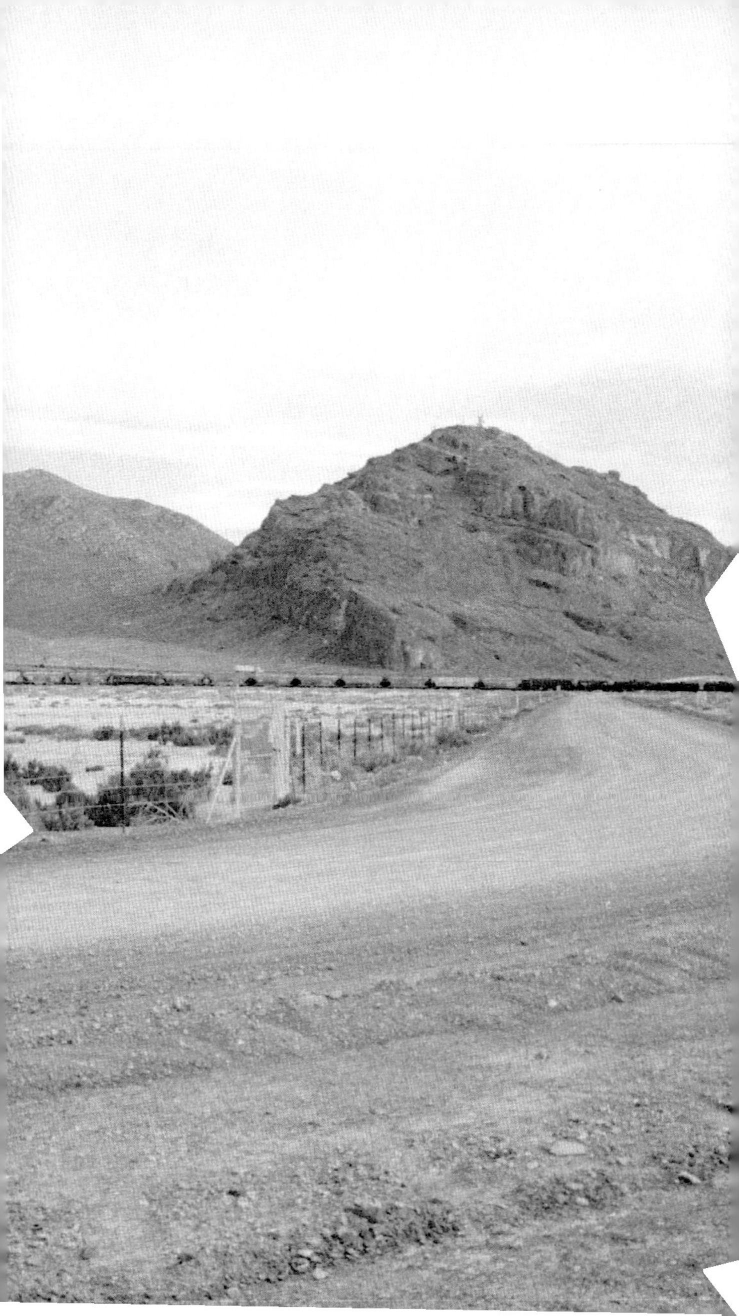

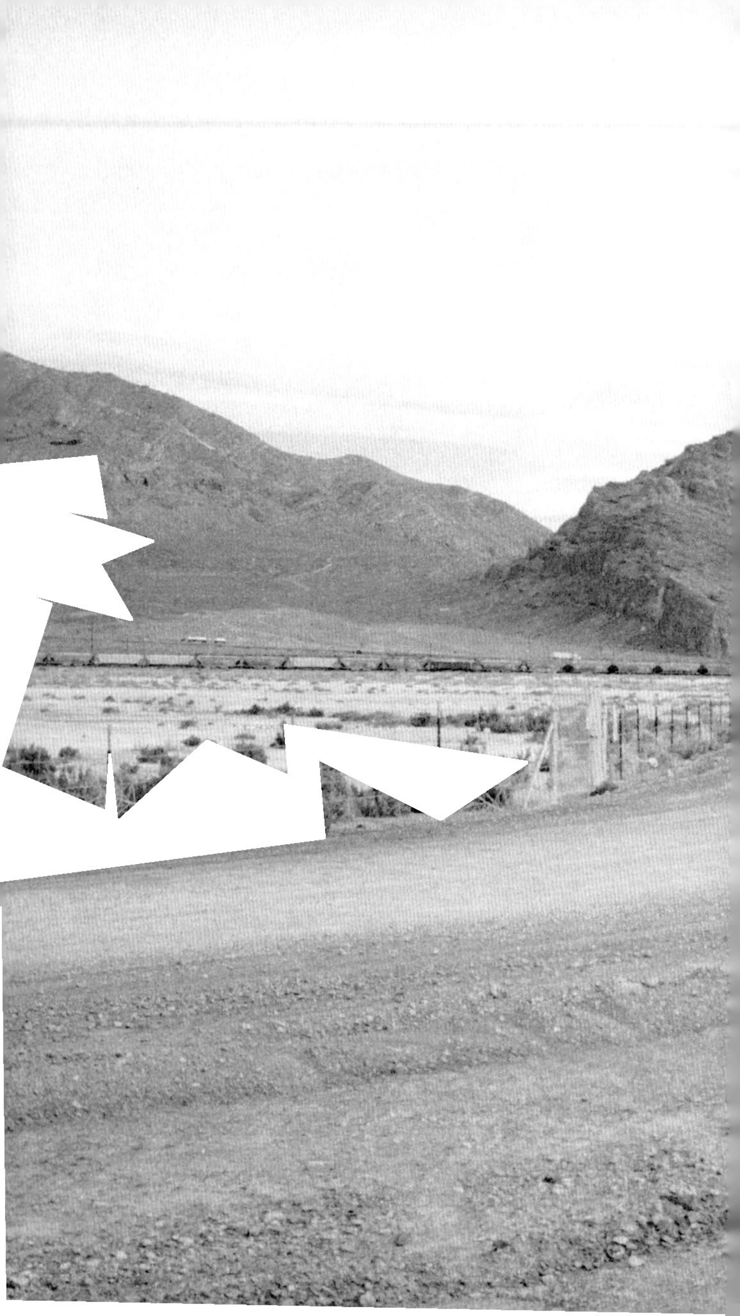

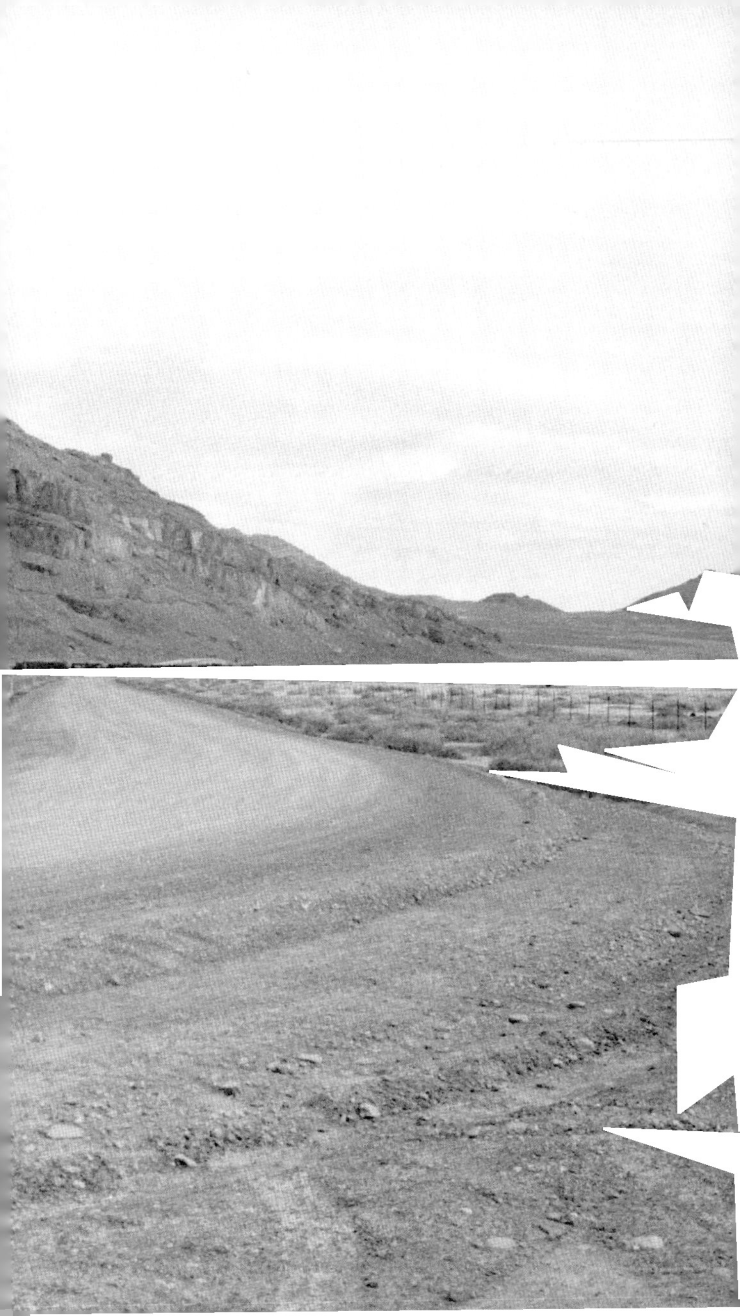

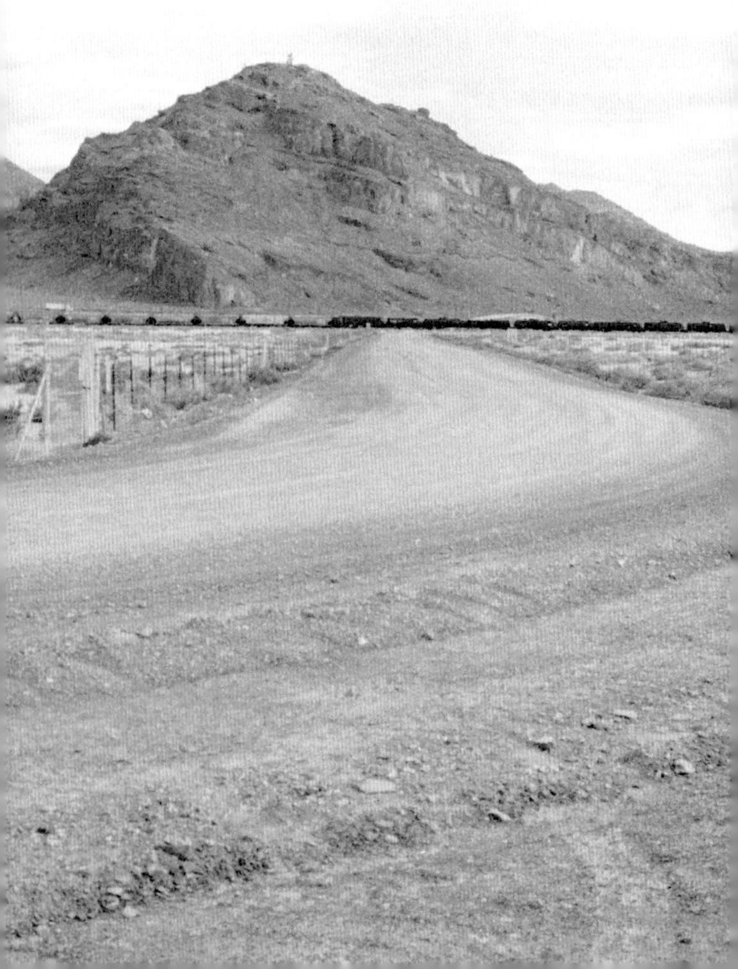

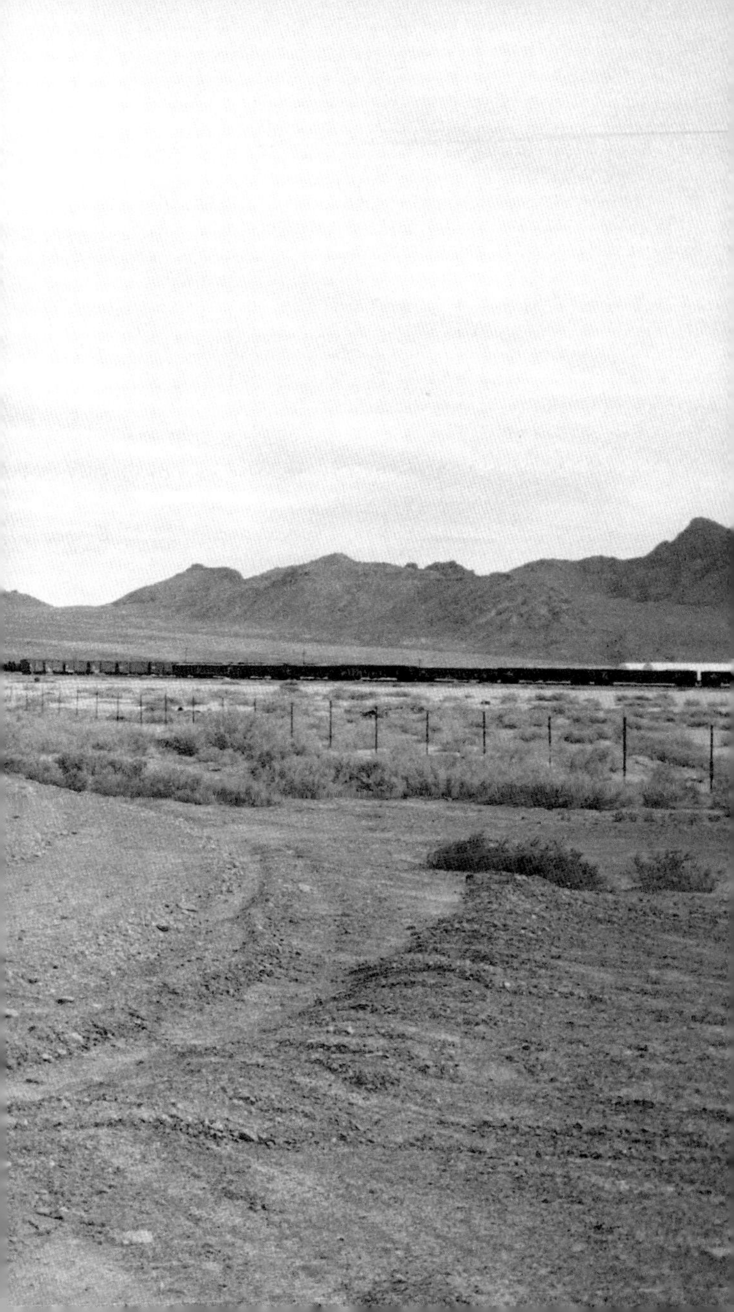

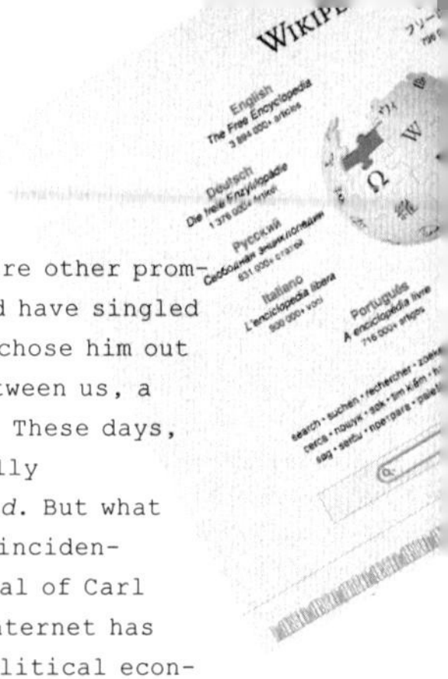

Was that too harsh? Obviously there are other prominent technology enthusiasts we could have singled out, so we hope Kevin understands we chose him out of affection. There's an affinity between us, a bond. After all, he blogged about us. These days, that's a direct connection, potentially a deeply personal one. He's our *friend*. But what does that word mean now, given the coincidental rise of Mark Zuckerberg and revival of Carl Schmitt? From our perspective, the Internet has turned "friendship" into a term of political economy. Most obviously we could point to the connections maintained across social networking sites: affiliations of varying professional and personal intensity, aided and abetted by communication technology but usually stemming from and sustained by face-to-face encounters.

There is, however, a second form of "friendship" operating online, one of greater concern to the present discussion, since it has become endemic to the web. It's *de rigueur* for magazines to offer mechanisms for registering semi-anonymous comments, if not entire user-profile systems. These features harbor the promise of virtual communities brought into formation by a publishing platform: passive readers become active participants; each article prompts a long chain of responses, a frenzy of productive conversation. The logic is appealing, yet we have been adamant in refusing to provide Triple Canopy readers with any such comment function. Even after our redesign, which further facilitated our connectivity to social-networking sites, there is no way to "talk back." Everything published is carefully edited, often elaborately produced, and properly attributed. As far as the website is concerned, Triple Canopy has only authors, no friends.

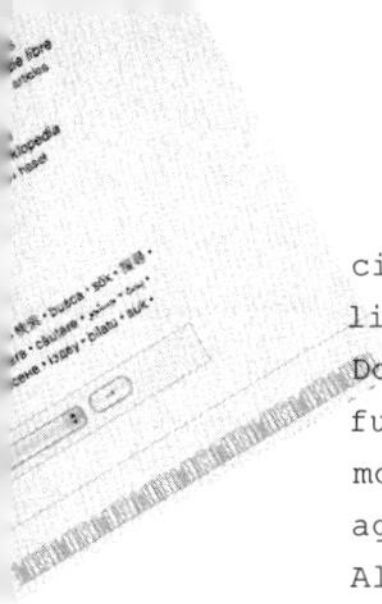

Is this where our crypto-reactionary tendencies become evident? Have we forsaken a forum for lively debate in the name of editorial control? Does our insistence on retaining a strong "author function" amount to a bid for authority, when a more progressive position might be to encourage what Foucault called "pervasive anonymity"?[8] All good questions, but, we suspect, flawed ones. They rest on the assumption that the Internet has the capacity to facilitate a truly democratic process: the more voices that can contribute, the more that may be heard, the greater our ability to arrive at a reasonable consensus, and so on. To put it bluntly, we're not sure this is a plausible description of our public sphere.

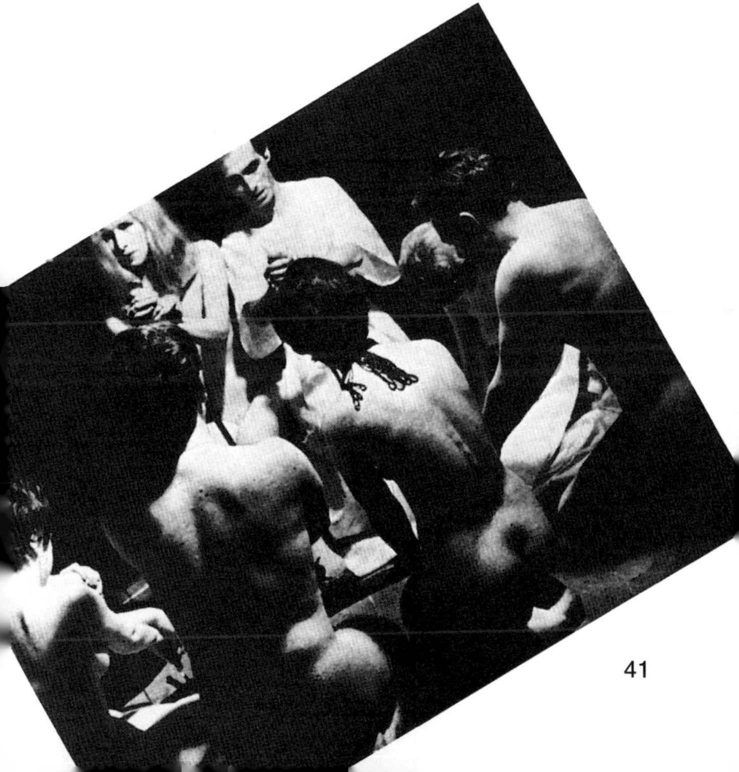

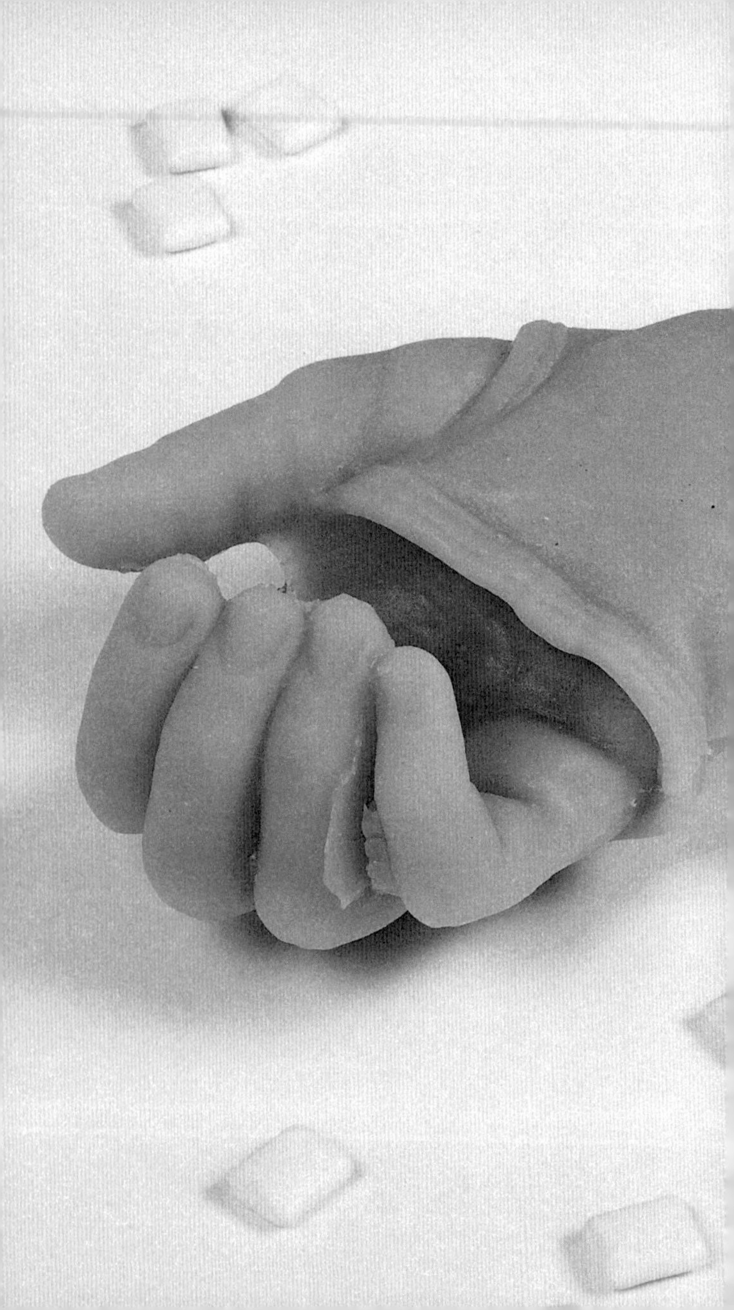

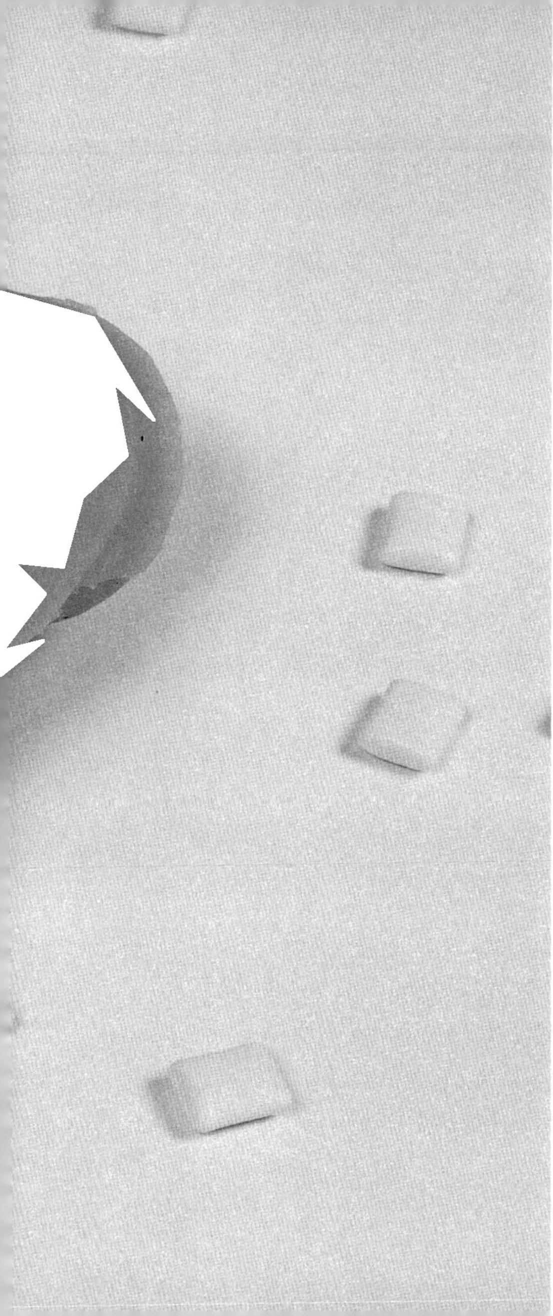

As the political theorist Jodi Dean argues, the proliferation of communication doesn't automatically enliven debate, but instead often forecloses it.

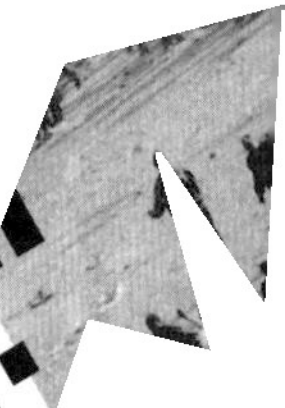

MULTIPLE VOICES DROWN EAC OTHER OUT,

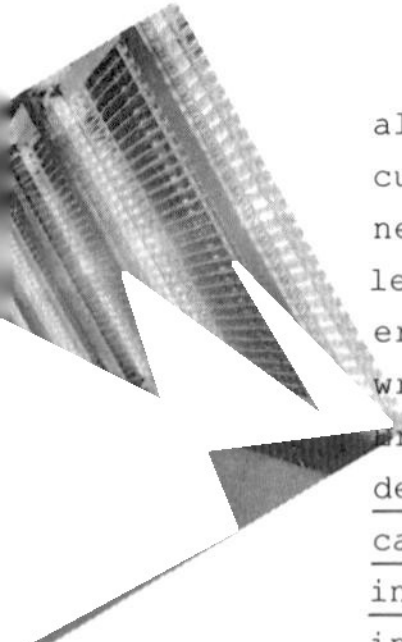

The resulting confusion favors those already in a position to exploit it. "The circulation of content in the dense, intensive networks of global communications relieves top-level actors (corporate, institutional, and governmental) from the obligation to respond," Dean writes. Drawing on the work of Chantal Mouffe and Ernesto Laclau, Dean argues that true democracy depends on antagonism, which is precisely what can't happen when messages zip past each other in frictionless circuits, when speech decomposes in a comments section. "There is no response because there is no arrival. There is just the contribution to circulating content."[9]

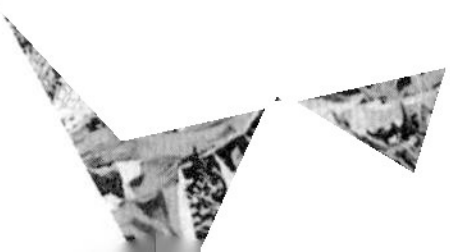

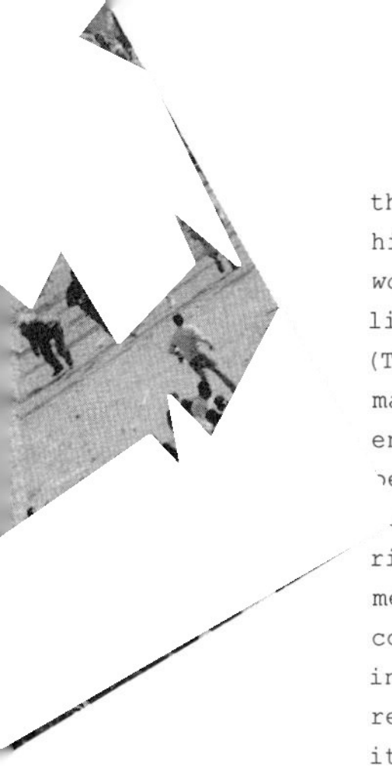

Obviously there are other takes on the Internet's communication surfeit. In his influential book *The Wealth of Networks*, Yochai Benkler writes off thinking like Dean's as "the Babel objection."[10] (That said, Benkler's relentless pro-market optimism that the Internet always enhances personal autonomy is hard to bear, let alone believe.) But if you buy Dean's analysis—and we sure do!—then the right approach to today's media environment is hardly to foster communication for communication's sake. If online publishing is to distinguish itself from the rest of the Internet's information stream, it mustn't settle for the easy terms of online friendship. It needs to maintain a degree of idiosyncrasy and difficulty. As a template for this, we've always looked toward the flip-books and fold-outs of *Aspen*, the magazine-in-a-box that so ingeniously coaxed its contributors into unfamiliar formats.

THE DREAM OF DIGITAL DEMOCRACY GIVES WAY TO PURE NOISE.

A productive friction came from reducing Tony Smith to paper sculpture, or committing Alain Robbe-Grillet to flexi-disc recording. *Aspen*'s appeal rested on these odd fusions of form, content, and author. To build a similar store of hybrid objects, we prefer to enlist writers and visual artists with little prior experience publishing online, and to expose them to the discomforts of a new medium. The result is a much more intensely collaborative process than any of us ever experienced in print—since it operates on the level not just of text and image, but also of code. Artists' proposals continually oblige us to consider what's possible, or even desirable, within the strictures of our platform. A contributor's original conception often hinges on a programmer's imagination. In contrast to the rapid-fire posting of most online content, our publishing process can be slow and protracted, with wrong turns and false starts that sometimes lead to confusion and disagreement. Dare we even say antagonism? We're afraid several of our past contributors would concur.

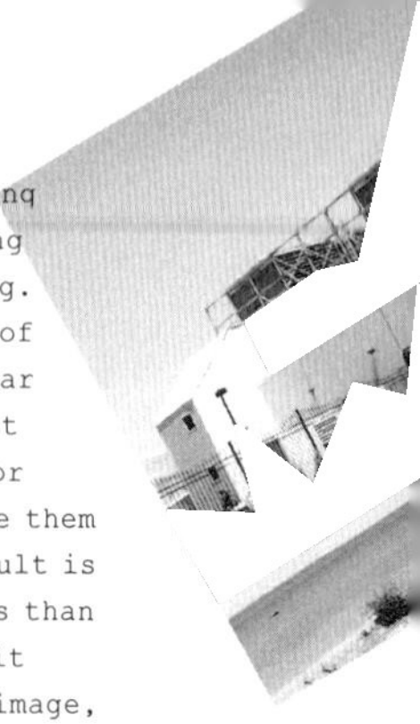

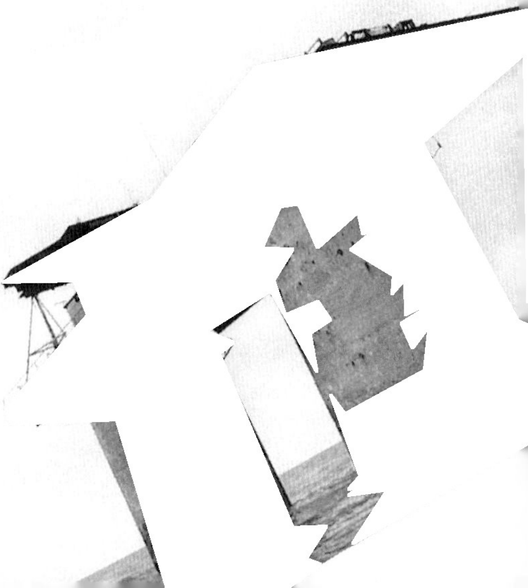

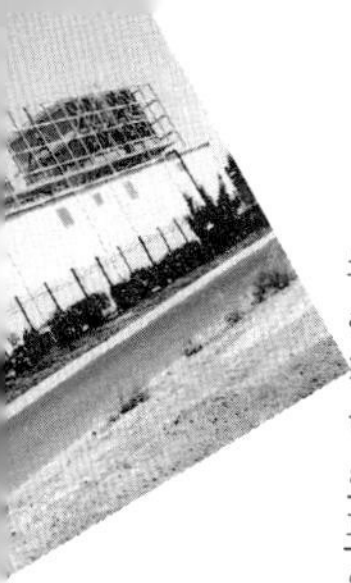

Of course, there is another vital distinction between authors and friends: authors are paid. (Inevitably and unfortunately, our honoraria are modest and meager, but still, they're some measure of regard.) Online friendship taps into a vast reserve of uncompensated labor—"friends" as outside contractors without contracts. For the *Whole Earth Catalog*, Stewart Brand encouraged readers to mail in product reviews and offered ten dollars for accepted submissions. Today, paying for reader contributions is such a rare practice that it sounds quaint and ludicrous, but it shouldn't. On this topic, Kevin Kelly is joined by a whole chorus of boosters—Benkler, Clay Shirkey, and Tim O'Reilly, to name just three—exulting in Wikiphilia. Certainly the achievement of Wikipedia warrants enthusiasm, but too often the example of this remarkable nonprofit endeavor shields for-profit ventures from tough questions about their attempts to harness the same collective energies. As for Triple Canopy, we've entered into enough potentially exploitive relationships ourselves that we're loath to further propagate any. We'll keep our consciences clear and keep signing checks. But doing so assumes a steady source of revenue—which obliges us to determine what sort of service we perform.

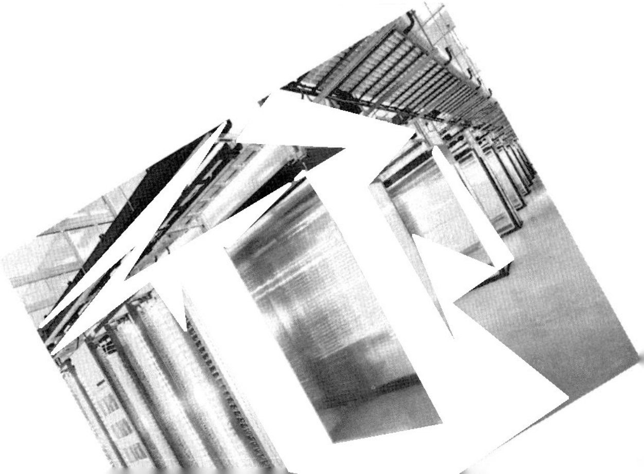

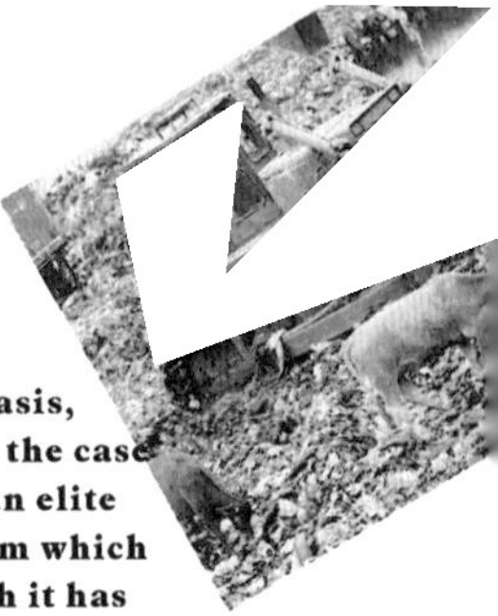

No culture can develop without a social basis, without a source of stable income. And in the case of the avant-garde, this was provided by an elite among the ruling class of that society from which it assumed itself to be cut off, but to which it has always remained attached by an umbilical cord of gold. The paradox is real.

—Clement Greenberg

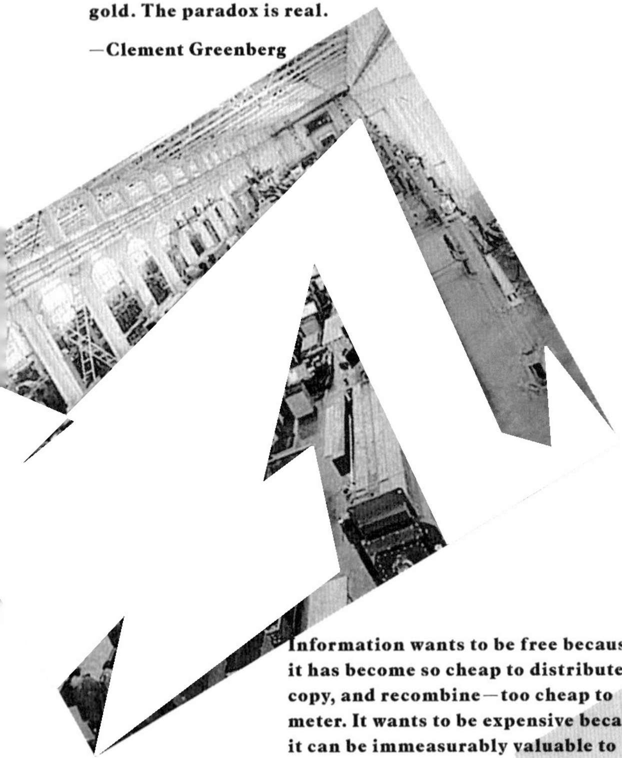

Information wants to be free because it has become so cheap to distribute, copy, and recombine—too cheap to meter. It wants to be expensive because it can be immeasurably valuable to the recipient. That tension will not go away.

—Stewart Brand

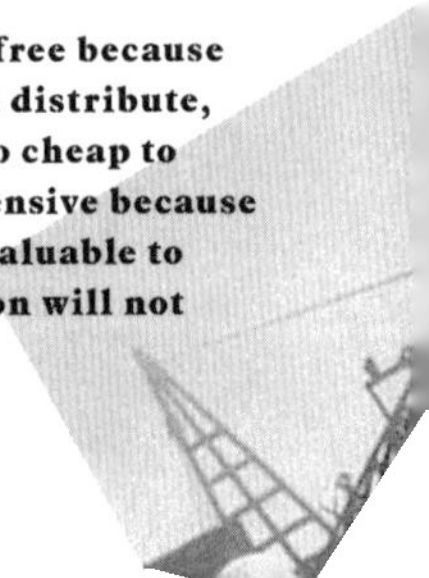

In 2009, after two years of running largely on sweat equity, Triple Canopy was selected to join a group of magazines supported by the Andy Warhol Foundation's Arts Writing Initiative, the first online publication to take part. The accompanying three-year grant, exceedingly generous, came wrapped in the slogan "capacity building"—meaning the foundation wanted recipients to spend funds in a manner that stood to improve their long-term sustainability. For the print publications in the group, this translated into developing sophisticated software tools for managing their databases and processing purchases, or campaigns to expand their subscriber pools. When we met with the consultant hired by the Warhol Foundation to evaluate our financial situation, it became clear we had few material needs, and even fewer obvious prospects for earnings; in terms of technical equipment, a few laptops and home broadband connections sufficed, and no one thought hawking suggested-donation drinks at release events qualified as a "revenue model." We convinced the Warhol Foundation that the best way to sustain Triple Canopy was to invest in human capital—quite simply underwriting a few part-time salaries so some of us could set aside the hours needed to pull together new issues, improve the website, apply for grants. We are forever in the Warhol Foundation's debt, but its support puts us in an odd position. The grant is in all likelihood the largest we will ever be awarded. As soon as the checks started to arrive, we had to consider how we would survive once they stopped. What's the revenue model for an arts publication that posts content for free on the web?

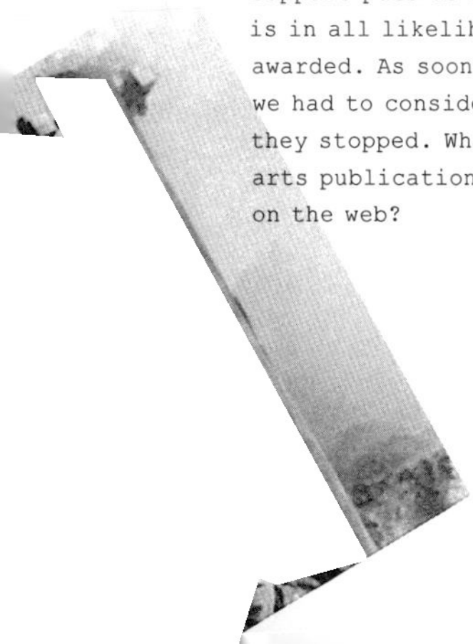

Wait, don't stop reading! We know, you're inclined to assume that a discussion of funding will be dull. But actually, as *Deep Throat* and *The Wire*'s David Simon have taught us, it's often when *you follow the money* that things get interesting. In the case of Triple Canopy, our current approach to sustainability frames a major conceptual issue for online publishing: the question of how to define an online magazine is still open-ended. To describe a print magazine, the postal service's criteria apply broadly: an assembly of printed sheets, dated and numbered, with consistency among issues and periodicity. You can fairly reliably identify a print magazine on the basis of a certain material construction and system of distribution. Employ the same logic to designate an online publication, and you wind up calling it a website that regularly, or semiregularly, posts new content—which applies equally well to the platforms of booksellers, law firms, restaurants, enterprising artists, or sixteen-year-old video-game enthusiasts. There's nothing specific to the design or dissemination of an online magazine, but nor is there anything constraining. We've elected to capitalize on this situation by behaving as several different organizations at once, and there's no sharper indicator of this than the diversity of our portfolio.

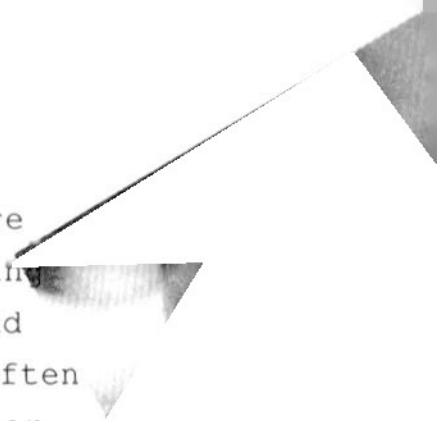

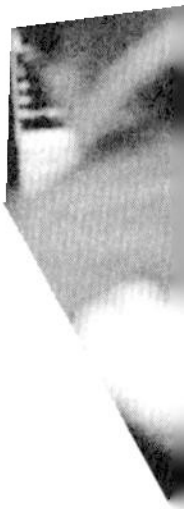

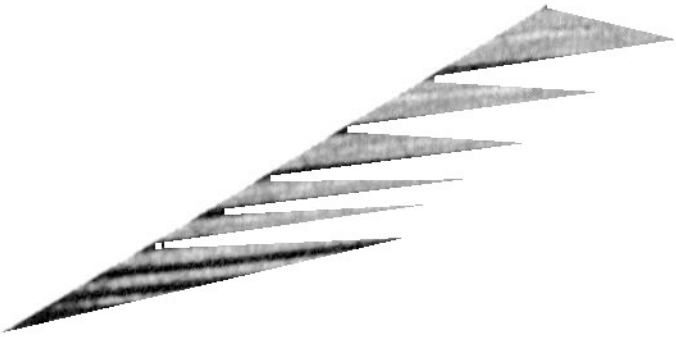

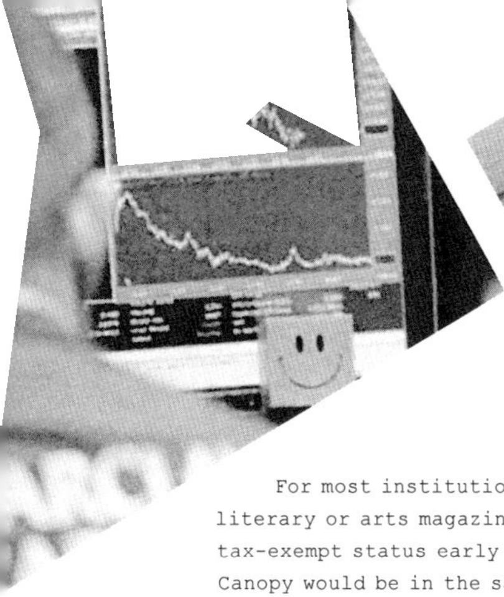

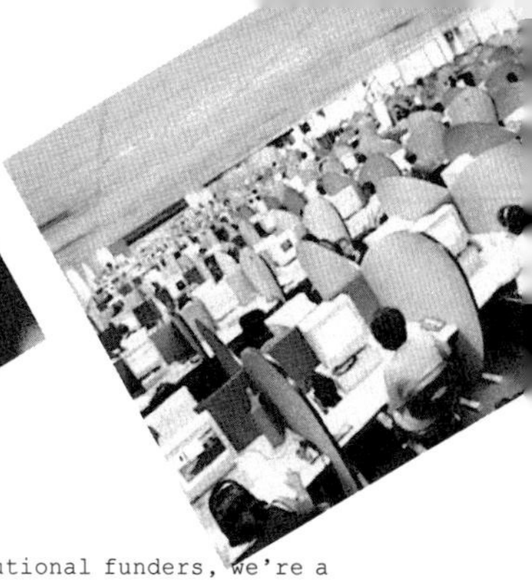

For most institutional funders, we're a literary or arts magazine. We filed for 501(c)3 tax-exempt status early on, assuming that Triple Canopy would be in the same financial sinkhole as many small print magazines; we had lower overhead, but we also had nothing to sell, so it would all level out at the same dismal bottom line. We hoped institutional support would alleviate the losses. But it's never been an easy fit. However inadvertently, grant criteria inevitably encourage specializing and serving precisely defined publics—stumbling blocks for a magazine with interdisciplinary interests and a geographically far-flung network of readers and contributors. So when preparing most applications, we narrow our purview. From the Warhol Foundation's perspective, we're an arts-writing publication, though one that hardly ever publishes writing about art; as far as the New York State Council for the Arts is concerned, we showcase poetry, short stories, and creative nonfiction by authors living within the state's boundaries; New York's Foundation for Contemporary Arts supports us for featuring new work by visual artists. Many of these applications are geared to specific projects, prompting the frequent atomization of our interests—hence one recent grant from Chamber Music America.

At the same time, we also operate according to the logic of a New York-based nonprofit art space. It's not such a stretch. From the beginning we've organized public programs at hosting institutions or temporary-occupancy spaces, and we continue to do so at our new office in Greenpoint. If the definition of an online publication is still so open-ended, we see no reason why it shouldn't exceed the screen. Indeed, organizing programs that fold back into content for the magazine, or vice-versa, has become our signal strategy for engaging with multiple publics. Virtually every arts organization uses a website to promote the activities going on in its space; we tend to do the inverse, holding programs in real space to promote what's happening on our website. And so we have emulated the fundraising "protocol" of venerable institutions like White Columns and Artists Space: we have a board of directors, form benefit committees, and proffer limited-edition prints. For our editors coming from a strictly literary background, these are completely alien rites; for all of us, they're slightly uncomfortable ones.

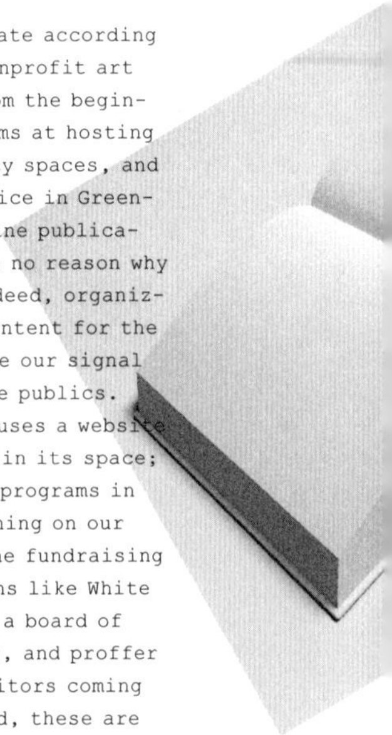

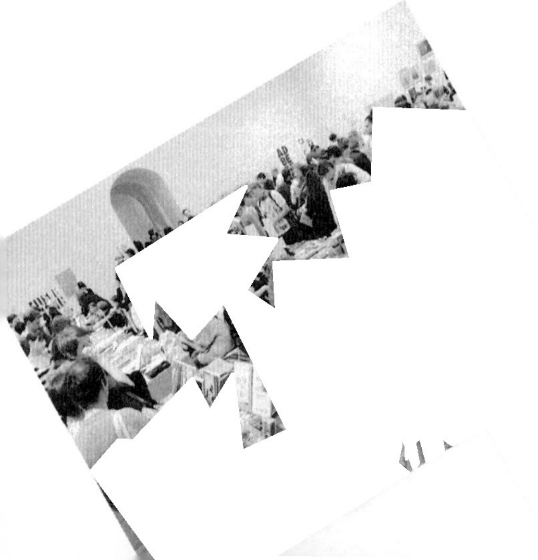

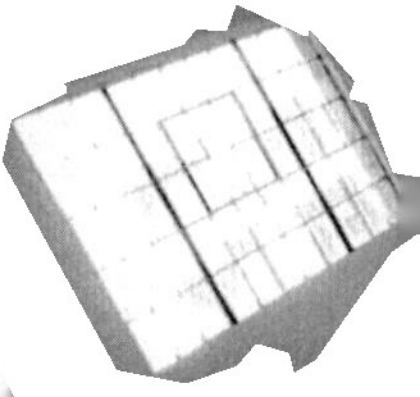

In short, our profile changes according to which set of funders we are addressing. And we have begun to address a third constituency, our readers, in a manner that we hope changes how they conceive of their relationship to Triple Canopy. Our readers have provided much in the way of moral support, but little of the material variety; for the sake of Triple Canopy's long-term sustainability, we believe some percentage of our public need to think of themselves as subscribers. Yes, we find ourselves in the same fix as Condé Nast, wondering how to encourage readers to pay for content we give away (only without resorting to the strong-arm tactics of subscription apps). It's a tough sell. Short of emulating the *Whole Earth Catalog* by running a tally of expenses on our website, it's hardly obvious how to convey a magazine's hard costs to a readership so accustomed to regarding information accessed online as part of the commons. We notice that our peers in print have responded to publishing's digitalization by doubling down on production value. A magazine like *Esopus* employs a rich variety of paper stocks, includes fold-outs and inserts, and lets loose a spate of typographic virtuosity. Each year we visit the New York Art Book Fair and marvel at the degree to which publications justify their cost through the ingenuity and craft of their material construction. Online, the same strategy suffers from a curiously reversed effect: the more exquisite the programming, the more the labor involved disappears from view. The ease with which our articles are accessed belies the amount of work that goes into their production. As we embark on a subscription campaign, it's not without irony that we're offering as an incentive our first book, *Invalid Format*, an anthology of past articles and related documentary material. So our bid for reader-based support of digital publication is centered on a printed object. The definition of an online magazine is both open-ended and contradictory.

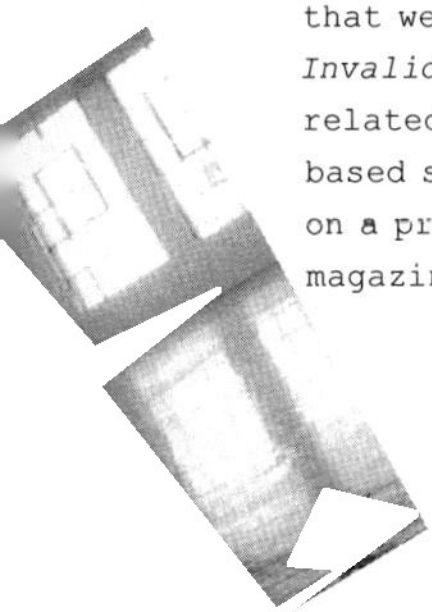

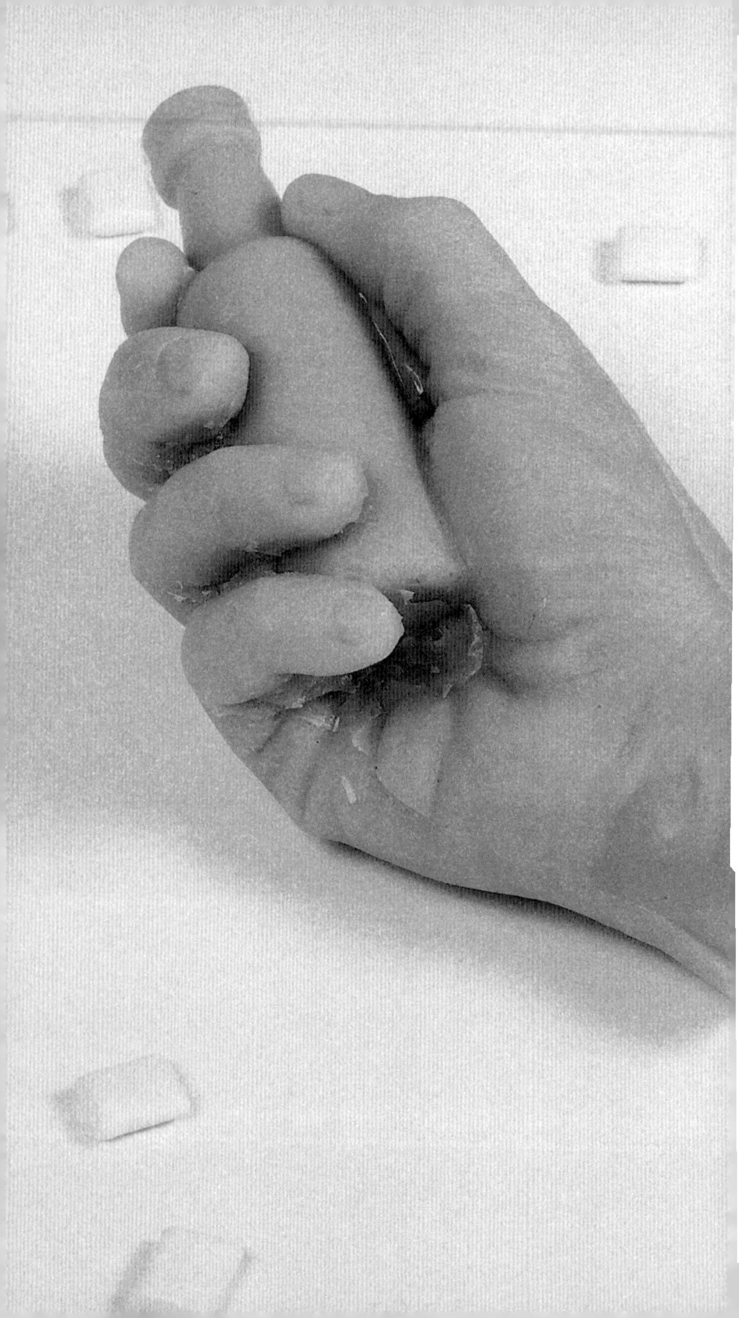

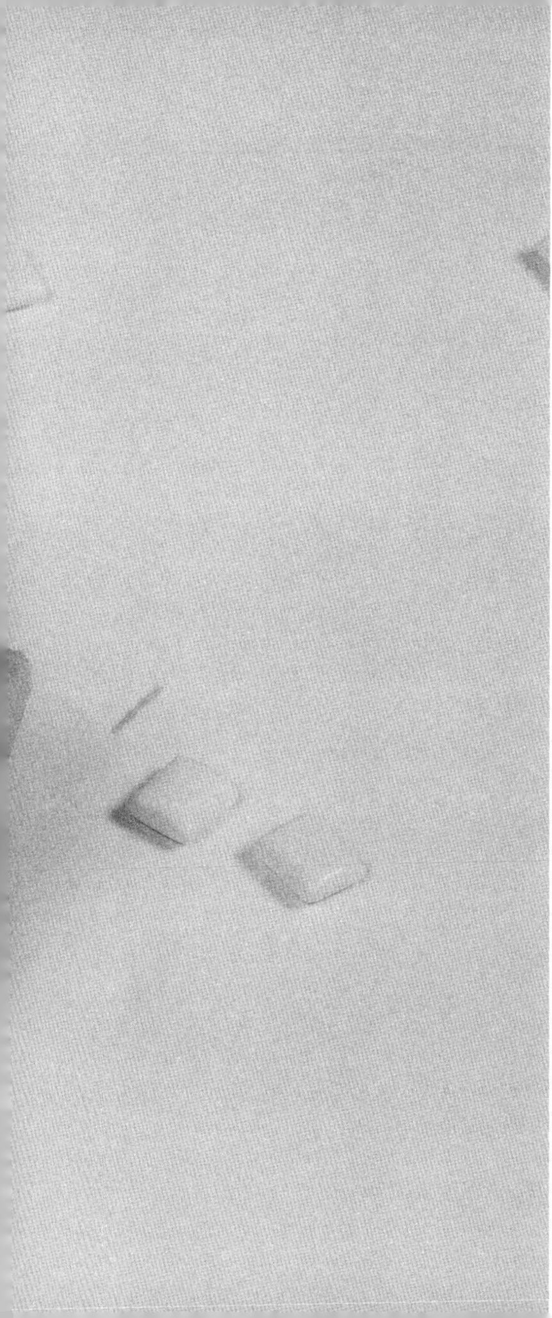

THE MORE EXQUISITE THE PROGRAMMING, THE MORE THE LABOR INVOLV DISAPPEAR FROM VI

We're hopeful for the subscription model, if not necessarily optimistic. As a first attempt at attracting broad support, we recently organized a Kickstarter campaign with Light Industry and The Public School New York to support our shared space in Greenpoint. We were heartened that 338 individuals pitched in, and grateful for the thirty-five thousand dollars raised. Yet we couldn't help noticing that nearly half that sum came from purchases of limited-edition prints by R. H. Quaytman and a unique artwork by Paul Chan, which we offered as rewards for upper-tier donations. Too often the rhetoric of diffuse participation masks the reality that capital remains concentrated.

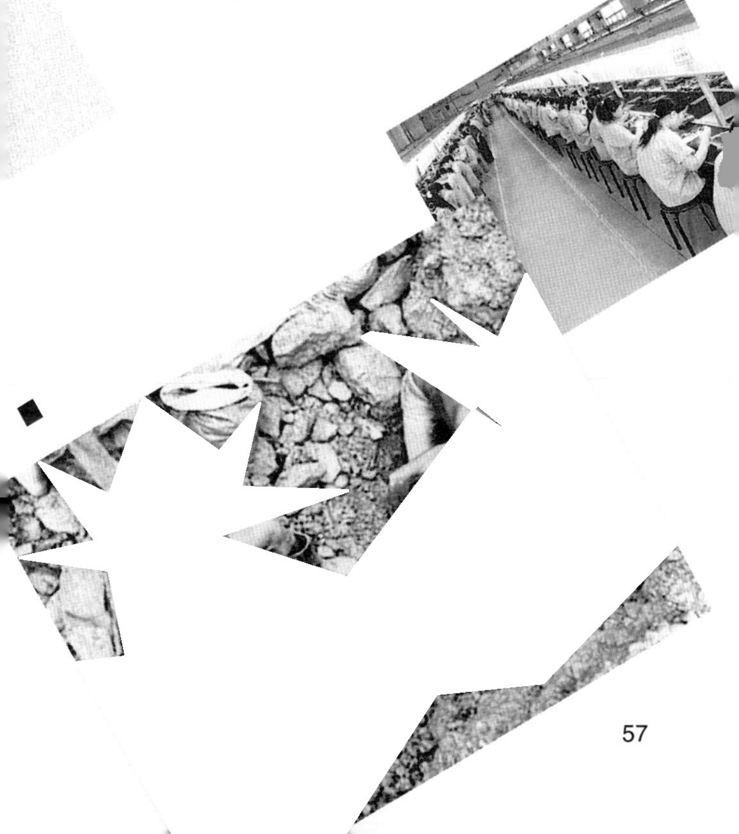

Rather than entrust ourselves to the generosity of readers, or to the continued largesse of funders who may themselves become casualties of the faltering economy, we're courting a fourth constituency, one that has emerged unexpectedly as a consequence of our online format: Since the release of our first issue, we have regularly received inquiries asking whether we do web design and development work. Which is to say there is a sizable contingent for whom Triple Canopy's website is neither a magazine nor the online presence of a nonprofit arts organization, but rather an advertisement for the skill sets of our staff. These requests have led to enough freelance gigs that we decided to consolidate them into TC Labs, which we describe as "a wing of Triple Canopy that works with clients to develop dynamic online experiences, innovative publication concepts, and generative public programs."

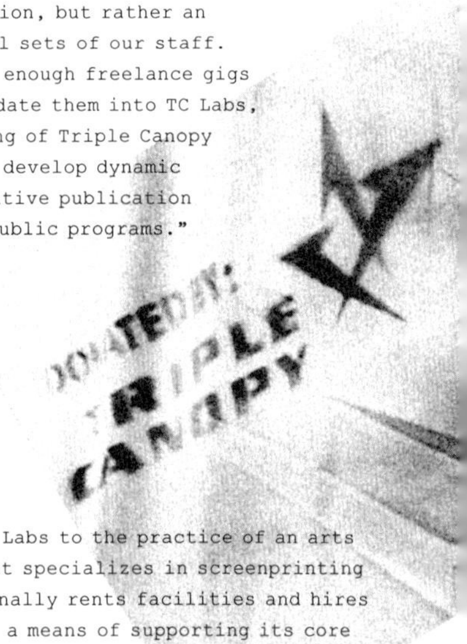

We liken TC Labs to the practice of an arts organization that specializes in screenprinting and that occasionally rents facilities and hires out personnel as a means of supporting its core mission. TC Labs represents an effort to monetize and reinvest the cultural capital accumulated by the project and its participants, and to wean ourselves off institutional funders. It's also the unexpected fulfillment of our cho-sen name: officially, we're contractors. The danger in metaphors is their propensity to turn literal.

Who are you a contractor for? It's not an easy question, though often the answer is obvious to everyone but you. Lackeys clamor for the privilege of working long hours in entry-level positions. Dividuals provide the data flow that Google channels through PageRank to generate enormous wealth for its shareholders. Friends contribute their labor *gratis* in the spirit of Wikiphilia, unrewarded but compelled by a bond of affection that often only goes one way. And mercenaries...well, at least they usually understand the terms of the agreement and insist on payment upfront. It's a confusing situation: we follow what we think are our own desires, yet it leads to the fulfillment of other entities' needs. When considering the shift from print to online publishing, of course there are substantial differences in the material supports, but the real issues emerge when you begin asking how information technology affects the exercise of power. In the conspiracy between human beings and techniques, whither digital publishing? Marshall McLuhan was right, the shift from typographic to electronic communication is epochal, but just beyond the Global Village is the Zone.

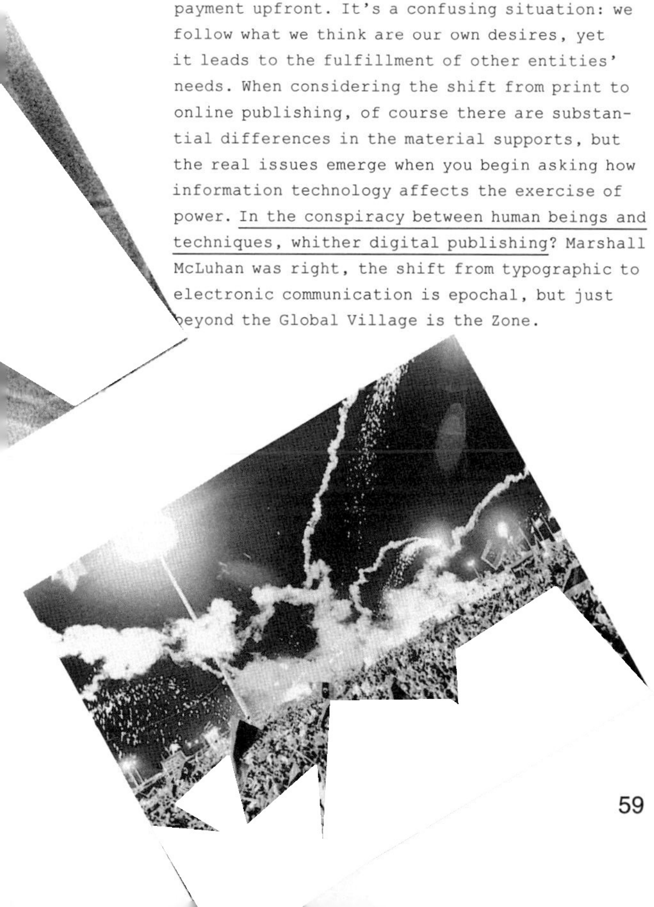

It's easy to get sidetracked—what with the analytics, the noise, the chatter from friends, the applications to funders, the freelance inquiries. This essay has made clear that Triple Canopy has definitely changed since we launched in 2008, in ways both subtle and substantial. You could say that's typical of any start-up, but you could also diagnose it as a peculiar strain of technological determinism: Our organizational structure, you see, matches the Internet's. As Galloway explains, the Internet is governed by two contradictory logics, one rigidly vertical (Domain Name System, or DNS), the other radically horizontal (Transmission Control Protocol and Internet Protocol, or TCP/IP). Likewise, Triple Canopy has a standard-looking (i.e., hierarchical) masthead, yet in practice we work in a decentralized, networked fashion, with clusters of editors collaborating on the individual projects (or nodes) that together comprise the magazine; those higher up on the masthead have committed more hours per week to Triple Canopy and as a result tend to be involved in more nodes.

We enjoy this manner of working, but certainly an organization with no fixed center is susceptible to drift. Without vigilance, Triple Canopy could fall victim to neoliberalism's imperative of infinite flexibility. This week a magazine, next week a design firm, or a curatorial initiative, or a murkily defined "consultancy." Maybe our appropriated name will finally cause sufficient brand confusion, and we'll find ourselves seriously considering a misdirected request for "logistical support" and a junket flight to Kandahar.

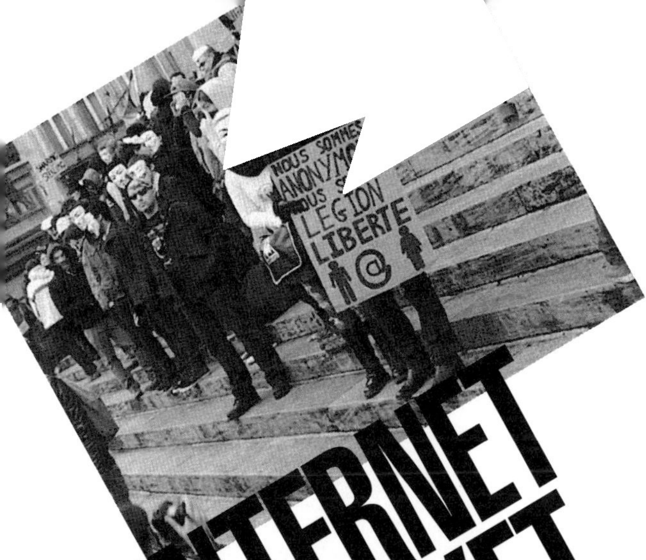

THE INTERNET IS A MARKET FOR NEW IDENTITIES.

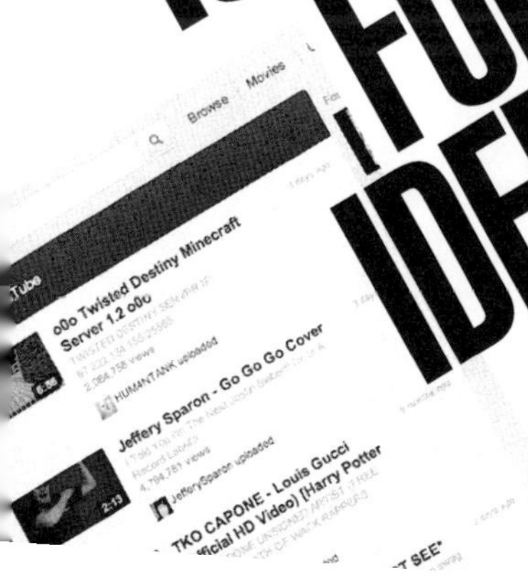

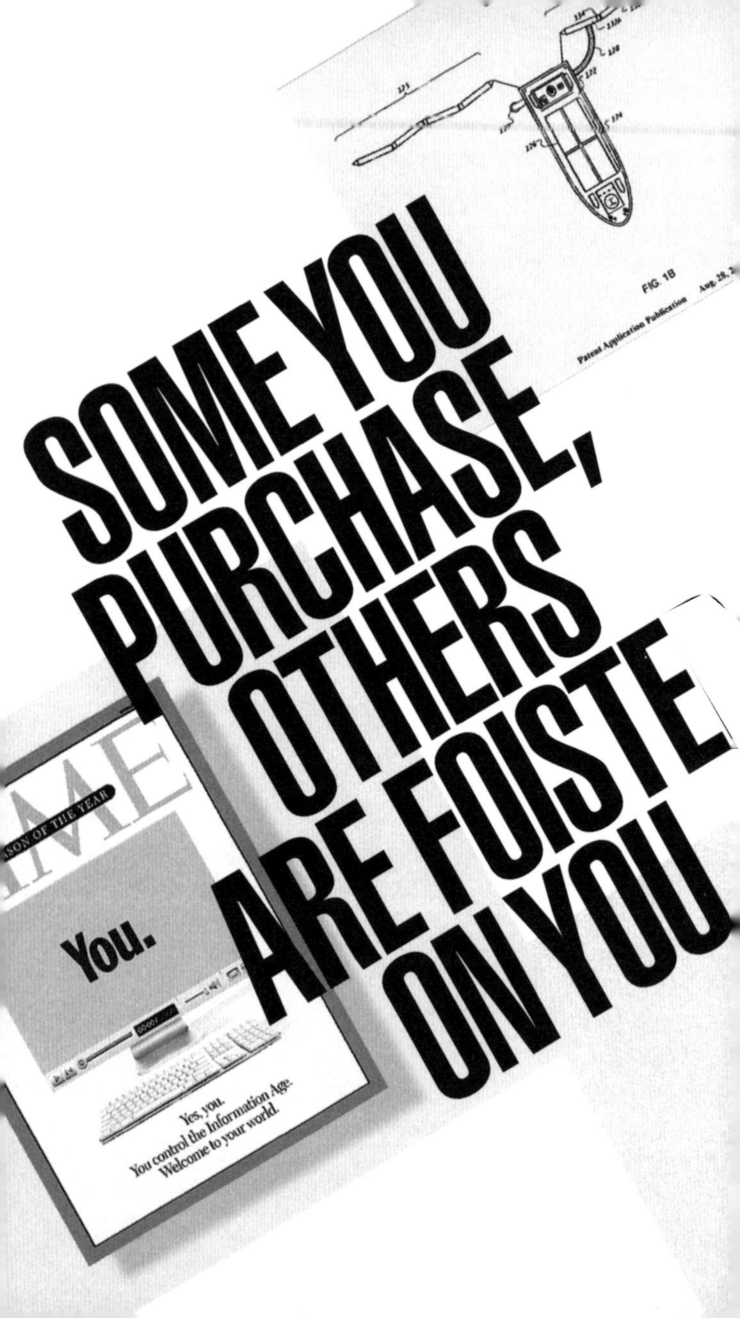

FIG. 1B
Patent Application Publication
SOME YOU
PURCHASE,
OTHERS
ARE FOISTE
ON YOU
You.
Yes, you.
You control the Information Age.
Welcome to your world.

Or Triple Canopy could simply come to an end, like many little magazines before—though it's not clear how that plays out, either. As a matter of individual staff members leaving, it's foreseeable enough: we'll accept teaching positions or writing gigs that pay better, or we'll simply grow exhausted of group meetings and the grind. But after the masthead collapses, what happens to Triple Canopy the magazine? When a print magazine folds, it stops publishing, and its back-issues languish on private shelves or lie in trash bins; the lucky ones reside in libraries as complete bound sets. Triple Canopy, on the other hand, will rapidly deteriorate: without preservation efforts, the website's source code will become buggier with each new upgrade of Firefox or the iPad; without payment of storage fees, individual pages will be wiped from servers, leaving only digital traces, dead links, rumors. Dispersal could be the media magazine's past and future. Perhaps it's prophecy that Phyllis Johnson published *Aspen* and then vanished from history,[11] just as Tyrone Slothrop, the putative hero of *Gravity's Rainbow*, gradually drops out of the plot and disintegrates. "He has become one plucked albatross. Plucked, hell—*stripped*. Scattered all over the Zone."[12] *Online*, of course! It was hardly a discussion. Little did we know . . .

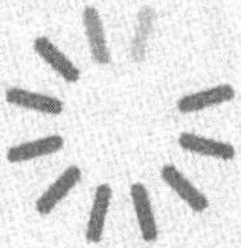

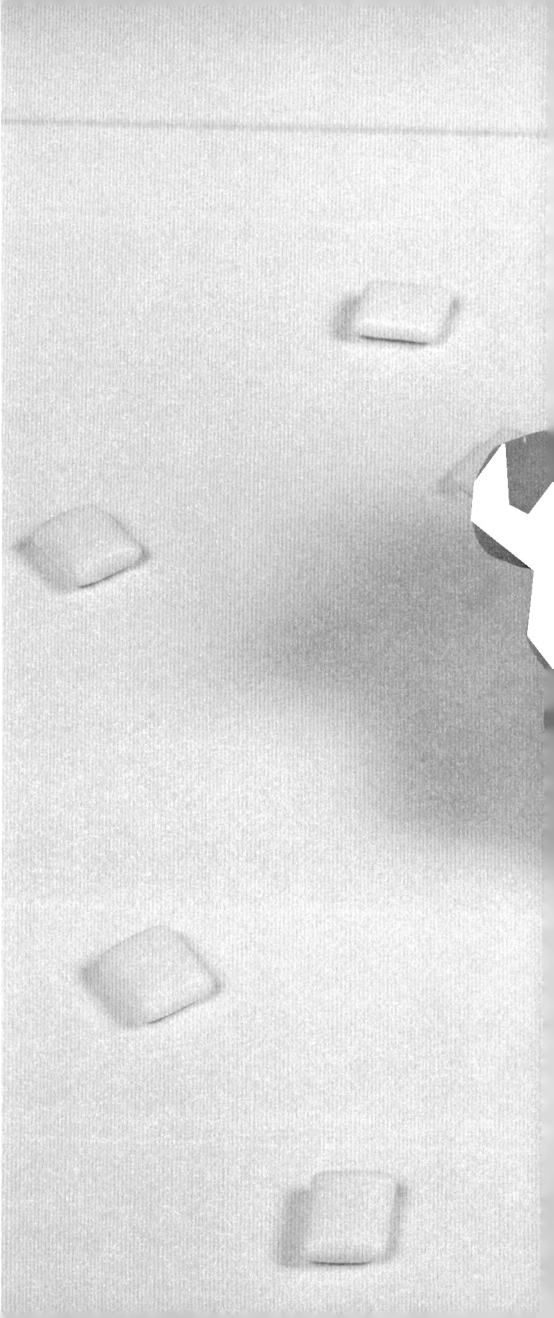

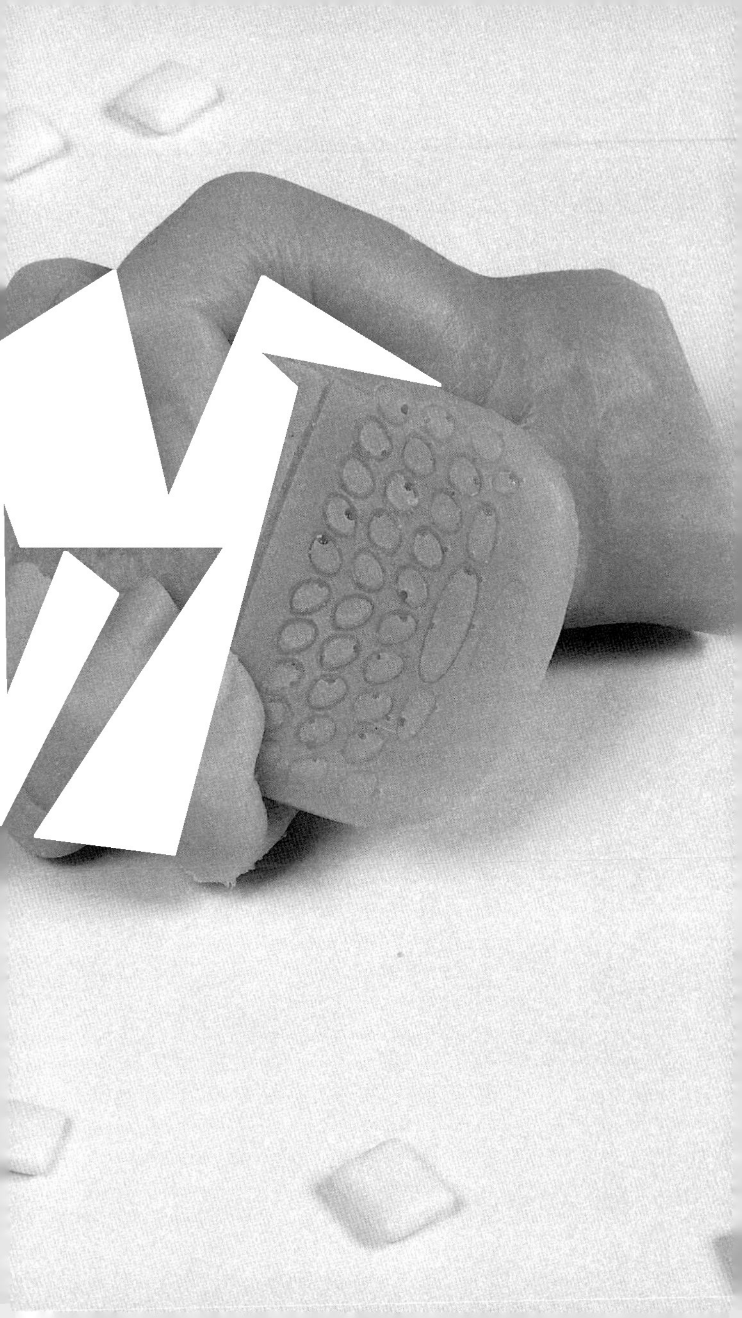

Works Cited

The epigraph is from Gilles Deleuze, "Postscript on the Societies of Control," *October* 59 (Winter 1992): 7.

1. Wyndham Lewis, "Blast Manifesto," *Blast* 1 (June 20, 1914): 30.

2. Alexander R. Galloway, *Protocol: How Control Exists after Decentralization* (Cambridge, MA: 2004), 142.

3. Deleuze, 5.

4. Galloway, 2004, 147, emphasis in original.

5. Kevin Kelly, *What Technology Wants* (New York: Viking, 2010), 17, 270, and 188.

6. Thomas Pynchon, *Gravity's Rainbow* (1973; New York: Penguin, 1995), 521 (italics and punctuation as in original).

7. See Fred Turner, *From Counterculture to Cyberculture: Stewart Brand, the Whole Earth Network, and the Rise of Digital Utopianism* (Chicago: University of Chicago Press, 2006), 90–91.

8. See Michel Foucault, "What Is an Author?" in *Language, Counter-Memory, Practice: Selected Essays and Interviews by Michel Foucault*, ed. Donald F. Bouchard, trans. Donald F. Bouchard and Sherry Simon (Ithaca: Cornell University Press, 1980), 113–38.

9. Jodi Dean, "Communicative Capitalism: Circulation and the Foreclosure of Politics," in *Digital Media and Democracy: Tactics in Hard Times*, ed. Megan Boler (Cambridge, MA: MIT Press, 2008), 102, 118.

10. See Yochai Benkler, *The Wealth of Networks: How Social Production Transforms Markets and Freedom* (New Haven: Yale University Press, 2006).

11. See Gwen Allen, *Artists' Magazines: An Alternative Space for Art* (Cambridge, MA: MIT Press, 2011), 67.

12. Pynchon, 712 (italics in original).

Artwork

Page 9. *Photographer's Hand with Digital Camera (Marcelo Gomes)*, 2011
pigmented silicone
4 ½ × 6 × 6 ½ IN — 11.4 × 15.2 × 16.5 CM
Edition of 5

Page 17. *Studio Manager's Hand with Advil Bottle (Margaret Lee)*, 2011
pigmented silicone
3 ⅛ × 3 ¾ × 6 IN — 7.9 × 9.5 × 15.2 CM
Edition of 5

Page 25. *Retoucher's Hand with Mouse (Jasmine Pasquill)*, 2011
pigmented silicone
2 ¾ × 4 ¼ × 6 ¾ IN — 7 × 10.8 × 17.1 CM
Edition of 5

Page 43. *Fashion Designer's Hand with Wrist Brace (Daphne Correll)*, 2011
pigmented silicone
2 ¾ × 3 ½ × 6 ½ IN — 7 × 8.9 × 16.5 CM
Edition of 5

Page 55. *Editor's Hand with Mini-Bottle (Ken Miller)*, 2011
pigmented silicone
3 ¼ × 4 × 8 IN — 8.3 × 10.2 × 20.3 CM
Edition of 5

Page 65. *Fashion PR's Hand with Blackberry (Cynthia Leung)*, 2011
pigmented silicone
3 × 4 ¾ × 6 ¾ IN — 7.6 × 12 × 17.1 CM
Edition of 5

Pages 34-39. Ore transfer road by intersection of transcontinental telephone, Internet backbone, interstate highway, railroad, and former microwave relay corridor. Air Force telemetry facility in foreground.

Photograph by Dan Torop (2011).

Mission & History

Triple Canopy is an online magazine, workspace, and platform for editorial and curatorial activities. Working collaboratively with writers, artists, and researchers, Triple Canopy facilitates projects that engage the Internet's specific characteristics as a public forum and as a medium, one with its own evolving practices of reading and viewing, economies of attention, and modes of interaction. In doing so, Triple Canopy is charting an expanded field of publication, drawing on the history of print culture while acting as a hub for the exploration of emerging forms and the public spaces constituted around them.

Triple Canopy was founded in 2007 as an informal, nonhierarchical, geographically dispersed editorial collective. A nonprofit organization, Triple Canopy currently consists of a staff of writers, artists, researchers, designers, and developers based in New York, Los Angeles, and Berlin. The magazine operates as the locus for the collaborative production of artistic and literary projects, research work, public programs, and print objects that mine the legacies of the artist book, the avant-garde journal, the political pamphlet, the alternative arts space, and the magazine-in-a-box, all the while enriching those forms with new media.

As a magazine, Triple Canopy is dedicated to slowing down the Internet. This begins with our design interface, which encourages prolonged, focused engagement. It extends to our methods: We work closely and collaboratively with contributors from the inception of a project to (and often beyond) its publication or public presentation. We consider the editorial process to be a collective enterprise, not a utilitarian transaction; a workspace for testing ideas and cultivating aesthetic experiments that might otherwise lack a critical, nonspecialized context, online or elsewhere. We are committed to learning from past efforts to rethink and renovate the print object and the exhibition space, as well as the literary and artistic forms they have engendered. We are convinced that the Web can act as a proper venue for these endeavors, one with its own materiality and timeliness.

Support

Triple Canopy gratefully acknowledges The Andy Warhol Foundation for the Visual Arts, The Brown Foundation, Inc. of Houston, The Buddy Taub Foundation, CEC ArtsLink, Chamber Music America and the Doris Duke Charitable Foundation, Experimental TV Center, Foundation for Contemporary Arts, New York City Department of Cultural Affairs, New York Council for the Humanities, New York State Council on the Arts, Office for Contemporary Art Norway, and the Orphiflamme Foundation, as well as the many individuals and in-kind contributors who have generously given their support.

Colophon & Credits

Published in the United States by Canopy Canopy Canopy, Inc., New York, 2012.

The Binder and the Server
By Triple Canopy
ISBN 978-0-9847346-1-0

Design by Franklin Vandiver
in collaboration with Triple Canopy.

triplecanopy

155 Freeman Street
Brooklyn, New York 11222
www.canopycanopycanopy.com

Triple Canopy is a nonprofit 501(c)3 organization.

For more information please write to contact@canopycanopycanopy.com.